The Macho Man Chronicles

Volume 1

By

Rob Whaley

All Artwork Generated by Rob Whaley

Copyright © 2024 by - Rob Whaley - All Rights Reserved.

It is not legal to reproduce, duplicate, or transmit any part of this document in either electronic means or printed format. Recording of this publication is strictly prohibited.

Dedication

This volume is dedicated to my family and friends, who continually support me in all of my crazy endeavors. To the positive thinkers. You know who you are. Give yourself a pat on the back.

Acknowledgement

I am deeply grateful to everyone who contributed to the creation of this book, directly or indirectly. Writing these stories has been a journey of imagination and dedication, and I owe thanks to several individuals and groups:

To my family for their unwavering support and encouragement throughout this creative endeavor. Your belief in me has been my constant inspiration.

To my father, Bill Whaley, who helped shape this idea for The Macho Man Chronicles. Over the years, we have had many brainstorming sessions. I listened to stories of your friends; you listened to stories of mine. We put stuff on paper. We laughed, we agreed, we disagreed. We made the invisible – visible.

To my mountain bike buddies, who listened to my ideas, offered feedback, and provided much-needed encouragement during moments of doubt. Your friendship means the world to me.

To my editor, Kevin Paul, whose keen insight and guidance helped shape these stories into their best possible versions. Your expertise and dedication to the craft of storytelling have been invaluable.

To the Substack readers and Grand Trunk Golf League dudes, whose feedback and constructive criticism helped refine each story and improve the overall narrative flow. Your perspectives were invaluable in making this book better.

To the literary community for providing endless inspiration, resources, and support to aspiring writers like myself. Your passion for storytelling fuels my own creative fire.

And lastly, to the readers. Thank you for giving these stories a chance, for immersing yourselves in the worlds I've created, and for allowing your imaginations to roam freely within these pages. Your engagement and support mean everything to me.

This book is the result of countless hours of imagination, hard work, and collaboration, and I am grateful to each and every person who played a part, no matter how small, in bringing it to life.

With heartfelt gratitude,

Rob Whaley

About the Author

Rob Whaley was born in *Martinsville*, Indiana, and now resides in South Central Michigan. He is a US Navy Submarine Veteran and alma mater of Purdue University and North Central College. In addition to writing, Rob is an avid mountain bike and gravel bike rider and competes in many of Michigan's famous mountain bike and gravel bike races, such as *The Iceman Commeth Challenge, Marji Gesick, Barry Roubaix and Mud, Sweat and Beers.*

Table of Contents

Dedication ii
Acknowledgement iii
About the Author v
Chapter 1: Drive Straight Through – The Machismo Scoring System 1
Chapter 2: The Mower Wars of White Oak Street 10
Chapter 3: Reel Warriors and The Need for Speed on Patoka Lake 15
Chapter 4: Iron Road to the Cup – The Grand Trunk Legacy 34
Chapter 5: Bowhunting Banter: A Tale of Machismo and Mockery 48
Chapter 6: Machismo Glow: – The Battle of Festive Titans 54
Chapter 7: Deer Camp Chronicles – Machismo, Mayhem and the Hunt... 77
Chapter 8: Tenderloins, Troubles, and Electric Connections: The Diner Chronicles 86
Chapter 9: When Machismo Meets Wokeness at the Woodward Dream Cruise 98
Chapter 10: Smoky Texas Bonds and the Legendary Weber ... 108
Bonus Chapter: Arlington Chronicles – Tales from the Links with Big Ray and Keith 119

Chapter 1:
Drive Straight Through – The Machismo Scoring System

The men traversed the rocky expanse of Stott's Creek, hopping from one stone to the next, their movements resembling a synchronized dance in the warm twilight. Joe Hamlin, a seasoned Navy veteran and machinist, led the trio with an eight-foot cane pole adorned with a Neptune—a tribute to the sea. Billy Baling, a millwright at a local transmission plant, swaggered behind, an ice bag heavy with freshly gigged bullfrogs slung over his shoulder, the National Ice logo in blue prominently displayed. Bobby Renfroe, a quality engineer, and Jim Humphrey, a union electrician, brought up the rear, each carrying their share of the night's amphibious bounty.

Stotts Creek, Green Township, Indiana circa 1980

As Bobby hopped from one rock to another, he exclaimed, "Bet you shit your pants, Billy, when you hoisted that fat bullfrog out of the water with that big-ass water snake attached?"

"Damn right," said Billy. "That was the darndest thing I have ever seen. Saved that sucker. Put him out of his misery. I'd rather take a gig to the head than get snake swallowed."

Joe, Jim, and Bobby chuckled.

Cikana State Fish Hatchery

The Cikana State Fish Hatchery loomed in the distance, its sprawling ponds teeming with aquatic life. The symphony of bullfrogs croaking, accompanied by the occasional splash, filled the air with a rustic serenade. The men, having conquered the art of frog gigging in the hatchery's vast waters, reveled in the success of their nocturnal escapade.

Following the easement behind the second row of the Willowbrook Subdivision homes, the scent of freshly cut grass enveloped them. Joe, reflecting on the escape from the mundane routines of work, couldn't help but feel the weight of the Neptune pole and the satisfaction of a successful night's gigging. The camaraderie forged in the moonlit architected ponds with willow-laced banks resonated with a simplicity akin to the prose of Hemingway himself. Joe's mind wandered, now understanding fully how his subdivision street got its name.

The group, now gathered in Joe's backyard, embraced the ease of a conversation punctuated by the metallic jingle of a bottle opener meeting the crown of a longneck beer bottle. The silver chain-link fence framed their haven, separating them from the vast cornfields beyond—traditionally "knee-high by the fourth of July." Stott's Creek meandered nearby, its gentle current providing a melodic undertone to the night.

In Joe's back yard, atop a concrete patio, he and Billy poured a few years earlier, sat a waist-high cedar table with ten-penny nails protruding, slightly stained from aged frog secretions, was a remanence of successful frog gigging sessions of summers past. A ball peen hammer, rusty lineman pliers and a filet knife rested on a lower shelf. Jim emptied half a ten-pound ice bag of freshly gigged frogs on the table.

Joe's backyard Green Township, IN circa 1980

"Ok to use these tools?" Jim inquired to Joe.

Joe exclaimed: "Marlene knew we would be successful, she put those there for us. Go right ahead, Jimbo."

Jim pulled a ten penny with the hammer claw, arranged a frog with his left hand, and the hammer in hand drove a nail through a bull frog's head. Laying down the hammer for the filet knife, he slit a bullfrog's skin just below its bulgy eyes. Using the lineman's, he gripped the tough green frog skin, pulling the skin down the frog's body over and off its legs in one clean pull.

"Damn, that was slick. Pro-Style," said Bobby. Jim looked toward Bobby with a half wink from his left eye and nodded, feeling appreciative that Bobby noticed the skill.

Amidst the frog cleaning led by Jim and Bobby, the machismo-laden debate surfaced once more—driving straight through from Martinsville, IN, to Tampa Bay. The challenge lay not only in the miles to be conquered but in the essence of the journey itself.

Joe, the undisputed advocate of the straight-through approach, proclaimed with unwavering confidence, "Gentlemen, driving all night is the only way! No wasted time, no dingy motels. Just pure adrenaline and getting there as fast as possible." His words were direct, unembellished, and carried the weight of experience.

Bill, the voice of reason in the group, countered, "Joe, I get your need for speed, but consider safety. Fatigue impairs judgment and reaction time. It's wiser to stop halfway and ensure a fresh start the next day." Bill's words, a counterpoint to Joe's bravado, echoed the pragmatic simplicity that defined his character.

Bobby, fueled by a determination to out-macho Joe, chimed in, "Joe, Bill has a point, but think about the adventure! Conquering fatigue, arriving in record time! Who needs sleep when you have the thrill of the open road?" His words resonated with an air of audacity, a challenge to the conventional.

Jim, caught in the crossfire between reason and bravado, cautiously suggested, "Guys, I see both sides. Risky to drive all night, but there's excitement in pushing limits. Maybe we could compromise and take short breaks?" His words, reflective of the internal conflict, embraced the nuanced simplicity of the group's friend set.

Joe scoffed at Jim's suggestion, "Breaks? That's for the weak! We'll power through, prove we're the kings of the highway!" His declaration, a manifesto of machismo, echoed the resolute tone often found in protagonists in many of his favorite authors' short stories.

"Almost forgot, I've got some fantastic 'gars my son brought back from his recent trip to Asia. These are the real deal, Cubanos. Joe, you'll appreciate this – Hemingway Short Stories." Billy then retrieved four short, robust-looking cigars from his cargo shorts pocket. After passing them to his friends, he pulled out a classic Zippo, bit the end from the cigar, spat the wrapper and pinch of tobacco to the side, and then opened the Zippo cover, creating a patented "clink" that echoed in the warm night air. Billy stroked the igniter wheel with his thumb. A thick yellow flame with a hint of blue at the base rose from the wick, indicating the lighter was well-maintained and properly fueled. The mesmerizing flame danced around the end of the stogey until it connected, producing a warm glow. Billy's jaws caved repeatedly, resembling a fish pucker, as he drew the rich smoke into his mouth, held it for a moment, and then blew a solid white stream into the night air. A second patented "clunk" sounded as he closed the legendary lighter.

"Greatest freaking sounds in the world right there. You know that click is probably one of the most recognizable sounds in the world. I heard the "click" sound is protected by a trademark." Explained Billy.

"No shit. What about the closing sound? What is that called?" Asked Jim.

"Well, the click is a no-shitter. But the clunk, not sure about that." Said Billy.

"I love the smell of the butane. And that cigar aroma, man that is like man-scent. We should make cologne from that. Cigar and butane," said Joe.

Billy, taking a deep draw from the Shorty Story, "Joe, it's not just about proving something. We have responsibilities to our families. They deserve a comfortable journey. Taking breaks ensures their safety." Bill's rationale, rooted in practicality, mirrored his grounded beliefs.

Bobby, mischief in his eyes, proposed, "A friendly competition? Joe drives straight through, Bill takes the halfway stop, and Jim and I switch positions every few hours or so to break it up. Let's see who comes out on top!" His suggestion, a blend of audacity and camaraderie, bore the hallmark of a machismo challenge. Bobby then lit his cigar, puffed, cocked his head upward and blew a near-perfect smoke ring that floated high above him. He looked over the Zippo, respecting the click and clunk it just produced.

"Nice hang time," exclaimed Joe. Bobby winked deep at Joe while nodding upward, raising the left corner of his mouth in perfect synch with the deep wink.

Concurrently, Jim's eyes widened, "A competition? That could add excitement, and we can experience both approaches. Count me in!" The spark of adventure in Jim's acceptance echoed in the warm night air. Jim rolled his cigar in his fingers, hand out, awaiting the Zippo from Bobby.

As the night deepened, the men realized the need for a quantifiable measure to settle their debate. Bobby, drawing from his work in quality engineering, suggested, "We need multiple metrics and a Likert scale to measure them. Like rate each category on a scale of 1 to 5, with five being the best. Then, total up the points."

Joe leaned forward, intrigued, "Oh, I get it, like one of those customer survey questionnaires. Is that what they call that numbering thing, a Likert? Sounds like some kind of critter."

Bobby, having polished off his first bottle of Miller Lite, belched, smiled, and said, "Exactly. We rate categories like Time Efficiency, Cost, Safety and Well-being, Experience and Enjoyment, and Documentation. The highest total score wins."

Jim, embracing the competitive spirit, asked, "So, we rate ourselves based on how well we adhere to each category?"

Bobby nodded, "Yep, and we calculate the scores at the end. The highest total score proves the best method."

Joe, Bill, and Jim, now armed with a scoring system, contemplated the categories and their implications.

The man gathered around the cedar table, establishing a bullfrog – the de-assembly process. Seamlessly sharing the ball peen, lineman, and fillet knife. Marlene had produced a few stainless-steel mixing bowls, which quickly filled with frog legs, while the ice bags filled with frog torsos.

*Joe's back yard. Willowbrook Drive,
Green Township, IN circa 1980*

"Thanks, Marlene. Would you mind getting some corn meal and some flowers and those grind-up-yourself salt and pepper shakers?" Jim asked as he sliced through a bull frog's skin with surgeon precision. Marlene nodded and said, "As long as you save some frog legs for me."

"Sure thing, honey," Joe exclaimed.

"Ok, to get the garden hose and clean these croakers up a bit, Joe," asked Billy.

"You know where she's at, Billy. Go right ahead," exclaimed Joe.

Bobby summarized, "On this scoring system, fella's Time Efficiency, Cost, Safety and Well-being, Experience and Enjoyment, and Documentation. Each rated on a scale of 1 to 5. We total up the points, and the one with the highest score is the winner."

Billy, raising his beer in agreement, added, "A fair and objective way to settle the debate. Let the competition begin!"

"You mean to let the frog leg cookin' begin, said Bobby to Billy. Beers were raised by all in agreement.

As the night unfolded, the men immersed themselves in the planning of their individual approaches to the road trip, cognizant of the impending scoring system that would quantify their exploits. They embellished in the delicacy of their bounty. The simplicity, clarity, and freshness of their collective idea permeated their dialogue, elevating their journey from a mere road trip to a literary adventure—a testament to the enduring spirit of the open road and the camaraderie it forges among those who dare to embark on its winding paths.

This story will be continued in a future separate short story. Be sure to subscribe to RobWhaley@substack.com – The Macho Man Chronicles for "Drive Straight Through" continuation and how the fellas scored themselves.

Chapter 2:
The Mower Wars of White Oak Street

On White Oak Street in Burlington, Illinois, four neighboring families lived side by side, forming an unlikely bond fueled by their love for their yards and the friendly rivalry that brewed between them. Larry Evans, a machismo man nearing his forties, took great pride in his meticulously landscaped yard. His lovely wife, Julie, and their two kindergarten-age daughters, Susan and Jody, added warmth to their picture-perfect home.

Behind Larry's abode lay the Burlington Township Park, a vast expanse of fields and trees. Dissatisfied with his lot size, Larry had secretly begun expanding his empire. Over the years, he had incrementally mowed beyond his property line, adding extra mower widths to his dominion. To cope with the increasing workload, Larry had recently purchased a John Deere riding mower, eager to claim a more beautiful lawn for himself.

During their usual gatherings in Jimmy Waltz's garage, fueled by beers and camaraderie, Larry regaled his friends with tales of his never-ending mowing endeavors. He complained about the Burlington Park District's neglect of the field, even jokingly suggesting that he might just claim it as his own.

Among Larry's closest neighbors was Robby Whalen, residing just a few houses down, across the street on White Oak Street. Robby's house also bordered a portion of the Burlington Park District, boasting a field and a pond. His beloved fox red lab, Hunter, was confined by a fence that guarded against unwanted escapades.

Behind that fence stood a sign, a reminder from the developer: "Do Not Disturb Wetlands."

Robby, too, succumbed to the allure of expanding his realm. Slowly but surely, he encroached upon the forbidden wetlands, one mower width at a time. With a garden, an apple tree, grapevines, and planters brimming with asparagus and potatoes, Robby believed he could repurpose the unused space. His mild machismo and slight egotism fueled his desire to conquer nature's boundaries. Robby, a Purdue University graduate, worked as a field service engineer at Motorola, while his wife Kristin, a University of Wisconsin graduate in political science, tended to their two boys and two girls.

In the vicinity, Danny Hendricks resided next door to Jimmy Waltz and his wife Michelle, content with their yard's beauty. As Jimmy continually assisted them in landscape improvements, Michelle relished the view of the park district field. A water drain line ran behind their lots, and Danny knew all too well the importance of maintaining a clean path for the water. With their two kindergarten-age boys, Lucas and Owen, Danny and Michelle strived to create a harmonious haven.

Danny, an IT manager at the Chicago Board of Trade, took pride in his role as the family's patriarch. Michelle doted on him, showcasing her culinary talents with evening meals and delicious weekend snacks and lunches. Danny's expertise lay in his mastery of meat smoking, and his barbeque skills had even led him to compete in the annual contests in Elgin, Illinois. Both Danny and Michelle had experienced divorce in their pasts, each bringing their sons from separate marriages to their new union. Budweiser beer was Danny's drink of choice, a comforting presence in his life, while Robby jokingly referred to it as "Mother's Milk."

Across the street from Robby and beside Larry, Jimmy Waltz, with his landscape architect degree from Iowa State, stood as the neighborhood's expert. Married to his high school sweetheart, Gilly, they had two little girls, Cindy and Penny. Together with his college roommate John, Jimmy owned a landscape company responsible for the remarkable transformations that graced the neighborhood.

Ironically, Jimmy's landscape crew unknowingly aided in the expansion of the neighbors' domains. While mowing Jimmy's yard, they inadvertently crossed the boundary, leaving behind a trail that crept further into the Burlington Park District with each passing visit.

And so, the Mower Wars of White Oak Street began, driven by a blend of machismo, friendly egotism, and an unyielding pursuit of the perfect yard. As these four men continued their mowing conquests, their satiric and amusing dialogue resonated through the neighborhood, their banter serving as a source of entertainment for all.

In a comical dance of lawnmowers, property lines blurred, and territories expanded, creating a tale of suburban absurdity. As the years passed, the rivalry between Larry, Robby, Danny, and Jimmy grew, and the legends of their lawn-mowing prowess became the stuff of neighborhood folklore.

Each man, with his idiosyncrasies and quirks, embodied the spirit of their unique households. Amidst the laughter, the challenges, and the ever-expanding lawns, these neighbors discovered that the true richness of life lies not in the perfect yard but in the bonds forged through shared experiences and the laughter that echoed down White Oak Street.

On a warm Saturday evening in the early 2000s, Larry Evans, Robby Whalen, Danny Hendricks, and Jimmy Waltz gathered in Jimmy's garage after a long day of mowing their lawns. The Chicago Blackhawks were playing in the Stanley Cup finals, and the four men were eager to relax, enjoy some beers, and engage in their usual banter.

Larry, his shirt drenched in sweat, boasted, "You guys won't believe the extra lawn I've claimed from that field behind my house. I've been adding to my empire one mower width at a time. The Burlington Park District doesn't stand a chance!"

Robby, sipping his chilled Budweiser long neck, raised an eyebrow. "Oh, is that so? Well, my friend, you should take a look at what I've accomplished. I've got my garden, an apple tree, and even some grape vines growing back there. It's practically an extension of my backyard."

Larry chuckled. "Garden and vines, huh? That's nothing compared to my perfectly landscaped yard. I've got lush green grass and vibrant flowers. I even bought a John Deere riding mower to speed up my mowing. I'm a lawn-keeping machine!"

Danny, grinning mischievously, chimed in. "Well, gentlemen, let me tell you something. While you're busy expanding your territories, I've taken the responsibility of maintaining the water drain line behind our lots. If that gets clogged, our yards will turn into swimming pools! I'm the guardian of drainage around here."

Jimmy, leaning against the workbench, interjected with a smirk. "You think you're the only one with extra lawn, Larry? My landscape crew accidentally mowed extra lengths into the park district each time. I've got the biggest lawn by default!"

The men erupted in laughter, each trying to outdo the other with their tales of mowing prowess and yard maintenance. As the Blackhawks scored a goal on the TV, they clinked their beer bottles together, toasting to their friendly competition.

Larry, pointing at the screen, exclaimed, "Hey, forget about the lawns for a moment! Did you see that goal? That's the kind of precision I bring to my mowing technique. It's all about finesse!"

Robby rolled his eyes playfully. "Finesse, Larry? I'm all about efficiency. I can trim and edge my lawn in record time while still enjoying a cold one. That's true multitasking!"

Danny, grabbing a bag of chips, chimed in, "Gentlemen, let's not forget the true heroes of our lawns—the wives. Michelle keeps our yard looking pristine, and I can't mow without her amazing snacks waiting for me afterward. She's the MVP of my team."

Jimmy nodded in agreement. "Absolutely, Danny. Gilly has an eye for landscaping, and she keeps our daughters entertained while we're busy maintaining our mowing empires. It's a team effort!"

As the game continued and the beer flowed, the men continued their good-natured competition, each proud of their lawns and grateful for their dedicated partners. Their Saturday evening tradition of machismo, satire, and humor would continue if the lawns needed mowing and the Blackhawks fought for victory. And so, the four friends enjoyed the game, the company, and the joy of being masters of their own suburban domains.

Burlington Gazette circa 2010: Impressionist painting from local artist RA Whaley

Chapter 3: Reel Warriors and The Need for Speed on Patoka Lake

The sun hung low in the sky, casting a golden hue over the tranquil waters of Patoka Lake. The air was thick with anticipation as Ronny Aubrey eased back on the throttle of his fully rigged-out Ranger, feeling the familiar rush of adrenaline coursing through his veins. Beside him, Billy Kidwell adjusted his cap, a wry grin playing on his lips as he surveyed the vast expanse of water before them. Billy reaches into the crumpled pouch of Red Man loose-leaf tobacco, his calloused fingers deftly navigating the familiar terrain within. With a practiced motion, he pinches a generous wad of the rich, aromatic tobacco between his thumb and forefinger, the earthy scent filling his senses with a comforting familiarity. Bringing the tobacco to his lips, Billy pauses for a moment, savoring the anticipation of the chew. With a slight smirk playing at the corners of his mouth, he tucks the wad into the side of his left cheek, the tobacco releasing its robust flavor with each subtle movement of his jaw. As he leans back against the boat seat, Billy closes his eyes, allowing the bold taste of the Red Man tobacco to wash over his senses. The smoky sweetness dances across his palate, a symphony of flavors that speak to the heart of his blue-collar roots. And then, with a satisfied exhale, Billy leans over the side of the boat, the cool breeze ruffling his hair as he spits a stream of tobacco juice into the water below. It's a ritual as old as time, a simple act that connects him to the land and the water, reminding him of his place in the world and the simple pleasures that make life worth living.

"They're gonna eat our wake today, Billy!" Ronny declared, his voice laced with excitement. "This bass mobile is a riggin' rocket, ain't she?"

Billy chuckled, nodding in agreement. "You bet, Ronny. This slick craft is a fishin' fortress, too. Can't wait to start flippin' and pitchin' around some of those secret structures near our honey holes. Those pro-fishermen won't know what hit 'em.. when they see us culling our well with hawg after hawg."

With a deft hand, Ronny maneuvered the Ranger, the massive outboard Mercury engine roaring to life as they surged forward, cutting through the water with effortless grace. The wind whipped through their hair, and the thrill of the chase electrified the air.

As they raced across the lake, the scenery blurred into a kaleidoscope of colors, the vibrant hues of the sunset painting the landscape in shades of orange and gold. Bald eagles soared overhead, their majestic wings outstretched against the canvas of the sky.

Behind them, Steph Allen and Roy Lindell followed in hot pursuit, their engine roaring as they vied for the coveted title of the fastest boat on the lake. The friendly banter between the friends filled the air, punctuated by the occasional roar of laughter and the excited whoops of triumph. Roy was famous for his war hoops, which he claimed he should patent – wooooohooo! He echoed across the lake. Ready to drop some shots in our honey holes, Stephy, my man. Whaddda ya say!"

"Hell yeah!" yelled Steph over the engine roar and wind turbine. "Love me some good blow-ups too. I want to run some top water shit. Hopefully, we be bagging a limit quick."

But amidst the exhilaration of the race, there was an undercurrent of determination that ran deep within the hearts of the four fishermen. They were not just racing for the sheer thrill of speed; they were racing for something far greater—a chance to prove themselves against the best of the best, to stake their claim as the champions of Patoka Lake.

As they neared their destination, the tension mounted, the air crackling with anticipation. The pro-fishermen awaited them with steely determination, their gazes locked in fierce competition as they prepared to do battle on the water.

But for Ronny, Billy, Steph, and Roy, the contest was about more than just winning. It was about camaraderie, friendship, and the unbreakable bond that united them as they faced the challenges that lay ahead. Known as the Bethany Bass Busters to their local friends, they had a reputation to live up to.

And as they crossed the finish line in a flurry of spray and foam, their boats skimming across the water with effortless grace, they knew that no matter what the outcome, they had already emerged victorious—victorious in the pursuit of their dreams and in the enduring spirit of adventure that burned bright within their souls.

Billy and Ronny: Courtesy of MLF Website

The Bethany Bass Busters

As the sun rises over the tranquil waters of Patoka Lake, the figure of Billy Kidwell emerges from the mist, a silhouette against the dawn sky. Hailing from the small town of Brooklyn, Indiana, Billy is a man of humble beginnings, his roots firmly planted in the blue-collar soil of the heartland. Despite the challenges he has faced in life, there is a quiet confidence in his step, a determination born of years spent toiling in the factories of Indianapolis.

Standing at an average height of 5'8" and weighing in at a solid 185 pounds, Billy's physique speaks of a lifetime of physical labor and dedication. His body bears the scars of his labor, the calloused hands and weathered skin a testament to the trials he has endured. But beneath the rugged exterior lies a keen mind and a fierce spirit honed by years of experience on the water.

Deaf in one ear from childbirth, Billy has learned to rely on his other senses to navigate the world around him. His eyes, sharp and alert, scan the horizon for signs of movement while his hands, steady and sure, work deftly with his fishing gear. A skilled fisherman, Billy takes pride in his craft, his bait-casting reels and graphite rods a testament to his dedication to the sport.

But it is not just skill alone that sets Billy apart; it is his deep understanding of the science and technology behind bass fishing that truly sets him apart from the rest. From weather patterns to water temperature, barometric pressure to fish habitats, Billy's knowledge runs deep, his expertise unmatched by many of his peers. In bass fishing slang, Billy's crew referred to him as a master at matchin' the hatch and patterning – picking the right lures for the appetite of the fish on any given day and understanding the specific factors such as water temperature and depth combined with lures that lead to successful catches. Matchin' the hatch was more of a fly fishing term, which Billy also was masterful, yet his friends carried this label into their bass fishing realm.

As he casts his line into the shimmering waters of Patoka Lake, Billy's mind is focused, his senses attuned to the slightest movement beneath the surface. For him, fishing is not just a pastime; it is a way of life, a passion that burns bright within his soul.

And as the sun climbs higher in the sky, casting its golden light across the tranquil waters of Patoka Lake, Billy Kidwell stands tall, a beacon of strength and resilience in a world filled with uncertainty. For him, the journey has only just begun, and the promise of adventure beckons on the horizon.

As the morning sun bathes Patoka Lake in a warm glow, three more figures join Billy Kidwell on the shore, their presence a testament to the camaraderie that binds them together.

First, there is Ronny Aubrey, a native of Speedway, Indianapolis, whose larger-than-life personality fills the air with laughter and excitement. Standing at 5'10" and weighing in at 220 pounds, Ronny cuts a striking figure, his beer belly a testament to his love of good food and fine beer. A skilled tradesman in the UAW and a former ironworker, Ronny's machismo lies not in his physique but in his passion for bass fishing. His full head of hair slicked back and glistening in the morning light, hints at a man who takes pride in his appearance, even as he revels in the rough-and-tumble world of the factory floor.

Next to Ronny stands Steph Allen, another bass fisherman and infamous UAW tradesman, his easy smile and infectious enthusiasm lighting up the morning sky. With a Ranger 375V equipped with a 150 HP outboard motor, Steph boasts of a speed machine that can top 70 mph on open water, his confidence in his abilities matched only by his love of the thrill of the chase. A fan of spinner baits and spinning rods, Steph's passion for fishing runs deep, his love for the sport evident in every cast and reel.

And finally, there is Roy Lindell, Steph's main fishing partner and a master craftsman in his own right. With his skillful hands and a keen eye for detail, Roy has built several fishing poles for himself and his friends, his expertise in rod and reel technology unmatched by many. A man of few words but great stories, Roy's tales of the one that got away are legendary, his ability to fabricate fishing gear a testament to his dedication to the sport.

Together, these four men stand united in their love of bass fishing, their friendship forged in the crucible of the factory floor and the tranquil waters of Patoka Lake. As they prepare to embark on their latest fishing adventure, their spirits are high, their laughter echoing across the lake as they set out in search of the ultimate prize—the thrill of the chase and the joy of victory.

Billy Kidwell: Courtesy of Patoka Lake News

The Announcement of the Patoka Hoosier Classic

As the anticipation for the upcoming Patoka Hoosier Classic builds, there's an electrifying buzz in the air, fueled not only by the promise of fierce competition but also by the exciting prospect of the event being televised by Major League Fishing (MLF). It's a groundbreaking moment for the local fishing community, as the MLF's interest in showcasing the contest signifies a recognition of the talent and passion that thrives in these waters. Unbeknownst to the local angles, the vision of the MLF was less emphasis on fish caught and more emphasis on the personalities, struggles, strategies, conflicts, and emotions of the anglers.

The announcement of MLF's involvement sends ripples of excitement through the fishing community, igniting the hopes and dreams of anglers far and wide. For the first time, the Patoka Hoosier Classic will be broadcast to audiences across the nation, shining a spotlight on the adrenaline-fueled battles that unfold on the tranquil waters of Patoka Lake.

The history of Major League Fishing serves as a testament to the transformative power of innovation and vision. Born from the shared aspirations of anglers and the Outdoor Channel, MLF was conceived with the goal of revolutionizing competitive bass fishing, presenting it to viewers in a fresh and captivating format. With its debut event at Lake Amistad in 2011, MLF captured the hearts of fishing enthusiasts and sports fans alike, setting the stage for a new era of professional bass fishing.

Now, as the Patoka Hoosier Classic prepares to make its mark on the MLF stage, the local anglers find themselves at the forefront of a thrilling chapter in fishing history. Their dedication, skill, and camaraderie will be showcased to a national audience as they go head-to-head against professional fishermen in a quest for glory.

With MLF's backing, the Patoka Hoosier Classic promises to be a spectacle like no other, blending the rich traditions of local bass fishing with the innovative spirit of modern competition. As anglers gear up for the challenge ahead, they know that they're not just competing for prizes and accolades—they're writing a new chapter in the storied history of their beloved sport. And with the world watching, they're determined to make it one for the ages.

Preparation and Strategy

With the announcement of the Patoka Hoosier Classic ringing in their ears, Billy, Ronny, Steph, and Roy set to work preparing for the challenge ahead.

Billy Kidwell meticulously inspects his bait-casting reels and graphite rods, ensuring that each piece of equipment is in perfect working order. He studies weather patterns and water temperatures, analyzing every detail to gain an edge over the competition. With a Texas-sized grin, he rigs his soft plastic worms "Texas Style," confident that his approach will yield results when the big day arrives.

Meanwhile, Ronny Aubrey pours over his beloved Ranger, his eyes alight with excitement as he upgrades the sonar system and fine-tunes the motor for maximum speed and performance. His beer belly jiggles with laughter as he regales his friends with tales of past victories, his machismo shining through as he boasts of his boat's state-of-the-art technology and chart plotting capabilities.

Steph Allen, ever the speed demon, revs up his Ranger, his foot itching to hit the gas and leave his friends eating his wake. With a wink and a nod, he declares that no out-of-state pro boat stands a chance against his speed machine, his confidence bordering on cockiness as he predicts a landslide victory for himself and his teammates.

And Roy Lindell, the master craftsman, busies himself with building custom fishing poles for each member of the group, his skilled hands working with precision and care. As he spins tales of the one that got away, his friends listen with rapt attention, their admiration for his craftsmanship evident in their eyes.

Together, the four friends share laughs and banter as they prepare for the contest, their camaraderie and friendship shining bright even in the face of fierce competition. With their equipment finely tuned and their strategies in place, they stand ready to take on the challenge of the Patoka Hoosier Classic, their hearts set on victory and their eyes fixed firmly on the prize.

Roy Lindell: Courtesy of The Bethany Gazette

Major League Fishing

As the Patoka Hoosier Classic gears up for action, the atmosphere crackles with anticipation as Maddie Dillard and Marty Rock from Major League Fishing take center stage, live-streaming their pre-tournament coverage. With the tranquil waters of Patoka Lake as their backdrop, they bring together the local heroes and the professional titans of the fishing world for a pre-contest interview that promises to be as entertaining as it is informative.

In the spotlight stand Billy, Ronny, Steph, and Roy, the hometown favorites with hearts as big as the Indiana sky, ready to take on the challenge of a lifetime. Opposite them are the seasoned pros, each with a wealth of experience and a trophy case to match, poised to defend their turf against the upstart contenders.

Maddie and Marty, with their infectious energy and quick wit, waste no time in getting the conversation started. With a twinkle in their eyes, they playfully pit the local anglers against their professional counterparts, stirring the competitive spirit that lies within each of them.

Maddie Dillard Interview with Billy Dancin: Courtesy The Fishing Channel

"So, Billy," Maddie begins with a grin, "how do you plan to outsmart these pro fishermen with all their fancy gadgets and gizmos?"

Billy chuckles, adjusting his Red Man tobacco pouch with a nod of appreciation for the challenge ahead. "Well, Maddie, it's all about strategy and knowing these waters like the back of our hands. We may not have all the bells and whistles, but we've got heart, and that counts for something out here. We practically live on this lake. We have our honey holes."

Meanwhile, Marty turns his attention to Ronny, a mischievous gleam in his eye. "Ronny, we've heard whispers about your need for speed on the water. Think you can leave these pros in your wake?"

Ronny grins, puffing on his cigarette as he leans back against his Ranger. "You bet, Marty. My boat may not be the flashiest, but she's got a few tricks up her sleeve. And besides, speed ain't everything—it's all about knowing what to cast and where to cast."

Steph and Roy, ever the dynamic duo, chime in with their own brand of machismo, regaling Maddie and Marty with tales of past victories and near misses.

"Now, let's hear from the pros," Maddie declares, turning her attention to the seasoned fishermen. "Billy Dancin', Babe, Texas Ted, what do you make of these local boys' chances? Are you feeling the pressure to defend your titles against the underdogs?"

The pro fishermen share knowing glances before Billy Dancin', with his rugged demeanor and weathered face, steps forward. "Well, Maddie, let me tell ya, these boys may have heart, but when it comes to reeling in the big ones, it takes more than just guts. We've been around the block a time or two, and we know what it takes to come out on top. But hey, may the best angler win, right?"

As the banter flies back and forth, the line between friend and foe blurs, replaced by a shared camaraderie forged in the fires of competition.

As the interview draws to a close, Maddie and Marty offer their best wishes to both the local heroes and the professional fishermen, their words carrying the weight of a community united in the pursuit of greatness. With the stage set and the stakes higher than ever, the Patoka Hoosier Classic promises to be a spectacle for the ages, a testament to the indomitable spirit of those who dare to chase their dreams on the water.

Let the Games Begin

With the sound of the starting horn echoing across the lake, the Patoka Hoosier Classic officially begins, and the waters of Patoka Lake come alive with the hum of outboard motors and the splash of lures hitting the water.

Patoka Hoosier Classic Start: Impressionist image by local artist Aunt Nano.

Billy, Ronny, Steph, and Roy waste no time getting down to business, their eyes scanning the horizon for signs of movement and their minds focused on the task at hand. With their bait-casting reels and spinning rods at the ready, they speed to their first honey hole then cast their lines with precision and skill, each angler determined to outdo the other and claim the ultimate prize. Billy gets a strike with a Texas rig and reels in respectable four pounder.

As the morning wears on, the competition heats up, with each team vying for the best fishing spots and the biggest catches. Billy, his non deaf ear tuned to the sounds of the water, expertly navigates his way through the maze of coves and channels, his instincts honed by years of experience on the lake. He is looking for some stained areas where the water is discolored by algae.

Ronny, his beer belly jiggling with every cast, works his magic with his Ranger, his upgraded motor purring like a kitten as he speeds from spot to spot in search of the elusive trophy bass. With his bait-casting reel in hand and a Texas-sized grin on his face, he casts his line with gusto, his machismo on full display for all to see.

Steph, his Ranger slicing through the water like a knife through butter, takes a more strategic approach, carefully plotting his course and analyzing every detail of the lake's topography. With his spinner baits and spinning rods at the ready, he casts his line with precision, his confidence unwavering as he waits for the telltale tug of a big bass on the line.

And Roy, his custom-built fishing poles in hand, works his magic with a quiet intensity, his skillful hands weaving intricate patterns in the air as he casts his line with precision and grace. With his vast knowledge of fishing rod and reel technology, he knows exactly what it takes to land the big one, and he's determined to prove his worth to his friends and rivals alike. Roy likes to drop shots, which is a technique of weighting a soft bait and presenting it vertically near the bottom of a water column.

As the day wears on and the sun climbs higher in the sky, the tension on the lake reaches a fever pitch, with each team pushing themselves to the limit in pursuit of victory. But for Billy, Ronny,

Steph, and Roy, the thrill of the chase and the joy of competition are all that matter. Their hearts set aflame with passion and determination as they cast their lines into the waters of Patoka Lake, ready to do battle with the bass and claim victory at the Patoka Hoosier Classic.

Overcoming Insecurities

Amidst the intense competition of the Patoka Hoosier Classic, moments of self-doubt and insecurity creep into the minds of Billy, Ronny, Steph, and Roy. Despite their outward bravado and confidence, each man grapples with his own inner demons, questioning whether he has what it takes to emerge victorious in the face of such formidable competition.

For Billy, the pressure to prove himself weighs heavily on his shoulders, his past insecurities stemming from his blue-collar upbringing and his deafness in one ear. As he casts his line into the water, doubts nag at the corners of his mind, whispering that he may not be good enough, that he may never measure up to the legendary fishermen he admires.

Ronny, too, feels the weight of expectation bearing down on him, his insecurities exacerbated by his beer belly and his penchant for smoking. As he speeds across the lake in his Ranger, doubts gnaw at his confidence, taunting him with the fear of failure and the specter of disappointment.

Steph, with his need for speed and his boasts of greatness, struggles to reconcile his outward bravado with his inner doubts, his insecurities lurking beneath the surface like hidden shoals. As he casts his line with practiced precision, a nagging voice whispers in his ear, reminding him that he may not be as skilled or as capable as he pretends to be.

Steph Allen: Courtesy of Patoka Lake News

And Roy, the master craftsman, finds himself grappling with feelings of inadequacy, his insecurities stemming from his inability to land the big one and his fear of letting his friends down. As he casts his custom-built fishing poles into the water, doubts cloud his vision, threatening to overshadow his confidence and undermine his resolve.

But amidst the turmoil of self-doubt and insecurity, the bonds of friendship and camaraderie remain unbroken, serving as a beacon of light in the darkness. As Billy, Ronny, Steph, and Roy cast their lines and reel in their catches, they draw strength from each other, offering words of encouragement and support and reminding one another of their shared journey and their shared dreams. With each cast and each catch, their insecurities begin to fade into the background, replaced by a sense of unity and purpose. For in the end, it is not the size of the fish or the number of trophies that matters, but the strength of the friendships forged in the crucible of competition and the knowledge that together, they can overcome any obstacle and achieve any goal.

Ronny Aubrey: Courtesy of Patoka Lake News

Triumph and Victory

As the final moments of the Patoka Hoosier Classic approach, tension hangs in the air like a heavy fog, the outcome of the contest balanced on a knife's edge. Billy, Ronny, Steph, and Roy feel the weight of expectation bearing down on them, their hearts pounding with anticipation as they cast their lines one final time, their eyes fixed on the water with laser-like focus.

With each passing minute, the stakes grow higher, the pressure mounting with every tug on the line and every splash in the water. The tension is palpable, thick enough to cut with a knife, as the friends push themselves to the limit, determined to prove their worth and emerge victorious against all odds.

And then, as if by magic, the moment of triumph arrives, a crescendo of exhilaration and pride that sweeps through the air like a tidal wave. With a mighty heave, Billy reels in a prize-winning bass, its shimmering scales glinting in the sunlight as he hoists it triumphantly into the air, a triumphant grin spreading across his face as he basks in the glory of his achievement.

Not to be outdone, Ronny follows suit, with the Ranger slicing through the water with precision troll motor propulsion as he reels in a bass of his own, its massive size a testament to his skill and determination. With a whoop of joy, he holds it aloft for all to see, his chest swelling with pride as he revels in the adulation of his friends and rivals alike.

As the final moments of the contest tick away, Steph and Roy join in the fray, their lines humming with anticipation as they reel in bass after bass, their faces alight with excitement and pride. With each catch, they defy expectations and prove their worth as fishermen, their spirits soaring to new heights as they revel in the thrill of victory.

And as the sun sets on the waters of Patoka Lake, casting a golden glow across the landscape, Billy, Ronny, Steph, and Roy stand tall and proud, their hearts brimming with pride and their heads held high. For in the end, they have achieved the impossible, defying the odds and emerging victorious against all expectations, their friendship stronger than ever and their bond unbreakable in the face of adversity.

Celebration and Reflection

With the final moments of the Patoka Hoosier Classic behind them, Billy, Ronny, Steph, and Roy gather on the shores of Patoka Lake to celebrate their hard-earned victory. The air is alive with excitement and anticipation as they await the announcement of the winners, their hearts racing with anticipation as they revel in the camaraderie and friendship that binds them together.

And then, as if on cue, the moment arrives, a chorus of cheers and applause ringing out across the lake as the winners are announced and the prizes are awarded. Billy, Ronny, Steph, and Roy stand side by side, their faces beaming with pride as they accept their accolades and bask in the adulation of their friends and rivals alike.

As they celebrate their success, the friends take a moment to reflect on their journey, their minds filled with memories of the challenges they faced and the obstacles they overcame. From their humble beginnings in small Indiana towns to their triumphant victory on the shores of Patoka Lake, they have come a long way, their bond stronger than ever and their spirits buoyed by the knowledge that together, they can achieve anything.

With a sense of gratitude and humility, Billy, Ronny, Steph, and Roy raise a toast to each other, their long neck Budweiser's clinking together in a gesture of solidarity and friendship. "Where is that bottle opener, Billy," says Steph. "I could not find it. I had to use my patent pending process to open ours." Steph hands the bottle to Billy. Billy grabs another unopened bottle from the cooler and holds it upside down, using the cap as a lever to pop the top on the other. "Slick," says Steph as he sees the cap pop off.

As the sun sets on the horizon, casting a warm glow across the landscape, the friends stand together, their hearts full and their spirits soaring as they reflect on their victory and look forward to the adventures that lie ahead. And as they gaze out across the waters of Patoka Lake, they know that no matter what the future may hold, they will always have each other, united by their shared passion for fishing and their unwavering belief in the power of teamwork, determination, and positive thinking.

Closing Scene

As the evening sky fades into darkness and the stars twinkle overhead, Billy, Ronny, Steph, and Roy gather around a crackling bonfire on the shores of Patoka Lake. The air is filled with the sound of laughter and camaraderie as they swap stories and reminisce about their triumph in the Patoka Hoosier Classic.

With the glow of victory still fresh in their minds, the friends share jokes and banter, their voices rising and falling in a symphony of friendship and joy. As fry a mess of morels in cast iron skillets over the flames and pass around a bottle of bourbon, they make plans for their next fishing adventure on the lake, their excitement palpable as they eagerly anticipate the thrill of the chase and the camaraderie of the open water.

And as the night wears on and the fire burns low, Billy, Ronny, Steph, and Roy sit side by side, their hearts full and their spirits high, knowing that no matter where their journey may take them, they will always have each other and the bond that unites them as friends and fishermen.

With a final round of laughter and a heartfelt handshake, they bid each other goodnight, their minds already turning to the adventures that lie ahead. For in the end, it is not the prizes or the accolades that matter most, but the shared moments of laughter and friendship that make life worth living.

And so, as they drift off to sleep beneath the starry sky, the friends dream of the adventures that await them on the waters of Patoka Lake, united in their love of fishing and their unwavering belief in the power of friendship to conquer all.

Chapter 4:
Iron Road to the Cup – The Grand Trunk Legacy

The recently graduated Michigan State alum, Kelvin Thomas Walters (aka by his friends as Kel or KT), had been anxiously awaiting the beginning of his first golf league experience, and now it was just about to start. As he clicked on the welcome to the new season email from a man everyone knew as "The Dicktator," he pondered why he had joined this league. He seemingly might be the youngest player in the league by at least 10-15 years.

The salutation read, *Good Morning, Golfers and Mr. Kowalewski.* The subject line read, *Welcome to the 2024 Season GT Golf League.* The email welcomed new members, had some housekeeping details, payment plans and an invite to PJ's pub on April 3rd for the official kick-off to its 50th consecutive season. From his understanding, the GT stood for Grand Trunk. He thought to himself, was this some kind of childish wordplay with the band Grand Funk Railroad? Kel then noticed a strange note in italics with some weird cryptic letters at the bottom of the email, which read:

"The Iron Road leads to Wisdom."

The Dicktator

Several weeks later, the sun shone brightly on The Mythos golf course near Rochester, MI, as Ron, Tony, Randy, and Kelvin gathered for their highly anticipated competitive round. The air was filled with machismo banter as each golfer boasted about their skills and equipment. This event had been in the planning for several weeks now, as the old wanted to properly welcome the new. Another chance to exhume their machismo, relish in the past, and remember what it was like to be young. Kelvin offered them this opportunity.

Ron Guzan, the self-proclaimed "Dicktator" of the 50-year-old Grand Trunk Golf league, proudly displayed his shiny new driver with the USGA maximum 460cc clubhead. Ron loved his nickname, as it was kind of fitting for his occasional dick head personality. He flexed his muscles, claiming that his distance off the tee would leave the others in awe. "You guys better brace yourselves for the longest drives of your lives!" Ron declared a mischievous grin on his face.

Tony the Greek, the seasoned scorekeeper of the Grand Trunk Golf League, stood confidently with his trusty putter by his side. He waved off Ron's taunts about distance, retorting, "Distance may impress the crowd, but accuracy wins championships. I'll be the one sinking those crucial putts, mark my words!"

Randy, a longtime member of the league, joined in the banter with a knowing smile. "Oh, Ron, always chasing the latest technology. But remember, it's not just about the gear; it's about skill and strategy. The Mythos is tight. Good luck keeping that big dawg in the fairway" Randy's calm demeanor masked a burning competitive spirit that he was eager to unleash on the course. "We all know you have GAS, Ron, not this stinky kind, you know, what I call Gear Acquisition Syndrome." The group chuckled in unison. "Never heard that one." Exlaimed Tony.

Kelvin, the newcomer to the league, listened intently to the banter. He admired Ron's impressive club collection but remained confident in his own abilities. "Wilson Fat shafts may not be the latest trend, but they give me the accuracy I need. And I've got a few tricks up my sleeve for chipping and putting," he said with a wink.

As the group gathered at the first tee, Kelvin couldn't resist kicking off the banter with a story from the prior week. With a mischievous grin, he recounted his recent adventure. "Hey, guys, you won't believe what happened to me last week," he began, a twinkle of excitement in his eyes.

"What now, Kelvin? Found a secret stash of golf balls hidden in the rough?" Ron teased, nudging Kelvin playfully.

"Nah, something even better," Kelvin replied with a chuckle and thought to himself to use a Yooper term meaning several beers in his story. "I stepped off the 18th tee to relieve myself of two-tree beers." He paused for dramatic effect, relishing the attention of his companions.

"And?" Tony prompted, intrigued by the buildup.

"Well, let's just say I stumbled upon a hidden treasure," Kelvin continued, his excitement growing. "I was relieving myself against this massive dead elm when suddenly, I looked down and saw a sea of gold all around me."

"A sea of gold? What on earth are you talking about?" Randy asked, his curiosity piqued.

"Mushrooms, my friends. Morels, to be exact," Kelvin declared proudly. "I called the guys over, and before we knew it, we were knee-deep in mushrooms!"

The group erupted into laughter, imagining the scene of mushroom hunting on the golf course. "You're kidding, right? Mushrooms on the golf course?" Ron exclaimed between laughs.

KT Morel Find

"No joke! We found about fifty of those beauties, all big and spongey," Kelvin confirmed, a sense of satisfaction evident in his voice. "We have been keeping it kind of secret, though. In talking with the course manager, she mentioned that the groundskeeper here was sort of cultivating them. Guess there are tons of shrooms in the woods here." Exclaimed Kelvin

"Well, I'll be damned. Who knew our golf course doubled as a mushroom haven?" Tony remarked, still chuckling at the unexpected turn of events. "Boys, just a reminder on the contest rules here. This is not just a lowest score wins here. Many ways to win. Most fairways hit, most greens in regulation, fewest putts, skins, low score each hole, low total score."

"How the fuck is that going to work, Einstein!" exclaims Ron.

"Simple. We assign points. Lowest total gets 5 points. Low score each hole gets 2 points. 2 points for a hit fairway, 2 points for a GIR. Skins will be a separate bet. Everybody in for $20 on the group of bets and $10 each for skin?" says Tony. Everyone nodded in agreement.

From that moment on, the banter continued as they made their way through the course, with Kelvin's mushroom discovery becoming the talk of the round. As they teed off, the camaraderie among the group only grew stronger, setting the stage for a memorable day on the links.

"So, what's up with those crazy green shirts you guys have with the naked guy putting?" asked Kelvin. "That is the one and only Mike Fucking Milton, "Tony replied. Ron jumped into the conversation. "Yeah, you got to meet Mike. So, last season, during the championship round, Mike was really hammered. He is in the last group coming in. Everyone is around the green waiting for the last group and hootin' and hollerin' giving Mike and DJ a bunch of shit. First, DJ mooned us all; Not to be outdone, Mike drops trough, walks on the green with shoes and shirt still on and puts for birdie – which he made. We were dying laughing. I almost fell over taking a picture, which is what Ron used to make the shirts".

"You guys are freaking nuts, just like the stories. Why I joined the league," – says Kelvin. "Well, you should fit right in then," exclaimed Randy in his soft and melancholy tone.

The group teed off, and the round began. Kel, teeing off last, noticed a peculiarity in each player's shot setups. Each of the three players tapped their driver on the ground 3 times in what seemed to be a specific rhythm. Each player meticulously recorded their shots, distances, and putts, ensuring an accurate account of their performance. Ron unleashed his oversized driver, launching a drive into the distance with power and enthusiasm, the ball drawing left towards the out-of-bounds wood line. He couldn't resist shouting, "That's a monster, train keep a rollin', stay on the tracks baby, follow the light." Miraculously and seemingly with a divine intervention, the ball stopped drawing; it landed next to the wood line and scurried up the fairway another 50 yards.

They progressed through the undulating terrain of Mythos Golf Course, navigating its extensive water hazards and the challenging up-and-downhill approaches to greens that varied in size and shape. Kel marveled at how the course truly captured its mythical theme, taking them through marshy wetlands and over long wooden bridge nature trails between holes. The rhythmic clicking and clacking of the golf carts on the bridges added an almost magical ambiance, making Kel feel as though they were traversing an ancient, enchanted land. Each golfer seemed attuned to the mythic topography, their focus and camaraderie deepening with every bridge crossed and every challenging shot taken.

Mythos Back Nine

Tony, meanwhile, showcased his finesse with pinpoint accuracy on his approach shots. He chipped and putted with precision, earning him satisfied nods from the others. "The short game is where it's at, gentlemen. In unity and precision, we find the cup," Tony remarked as he sank a challenging putt. Kel, while thinking Tony's last comment odd, also noticed an interesting engraving on the top of Tony's putter which at a distance appeared to be a gear with a small flame inside it.

Tony's Mysterious Putter

Randy's steady play impressed the group, his consistent swings maintaining a respectable pace. Although his health had declined, his determination to compete remained unwavering. He silently observed the banter, knowing that actions spoke louder than words.

Kelvin surprised everyone with his impressive performance. His fat shaft irons proved to be more accurate than expected, and his Trusty Rusty wedges lived up to their name. He matched Ron's distances with his driver, leaving the "Dicktator" momentarily speechless.

After the round, the group reconvened at PJ's Pub, their favorite gathering spot. Beers were ordered, and scorecards were examined with eager anticipation. Ron, slightly humbled by Kelvin's performance, admitted, "Alright, Kelvin, you've got some serious game. Those fat shafts are working for you."

Tony, ever the data-driven golfer, analyzed the scores and distances with a thoughtful expression. "It seems accuracy and strategy prevailed today, gentlemen. The results speak for themselves," he concluded, giving Kelvin a nod of approval.

Randy, content with his solid performance, smiled at the camaraderie shared by the group. "No matter how much we tease and challenge each other, we're all here for the love of the game," he remarked, raising his glass in a toast.

Kelvin pondered his last week's match and conversation with Rod, a retired Grand Trunk Railroad worker and over 40-year veteran of the Grand Talk Golf League.

Kel adjusted his cap and turned to Rod.

"So, Rod, I've been hearing a lot about the founding members of this league. Larry Carlisle, he was one of the originals, right?" Rod chuckled, swinging his club idly. "Oh, Larry? Yeah, he was one of the originals. Quite the character, that one. Always had a knack for making things... interesting."

"Interesting how?" Kel asked, curious.

Rod gave a sly smile. "Well, Larry was into all sorts of stuff. He'd always bring these old books and talk about secret societies and ancient symbols. Some of us thought he was just pulling our leg, but he took it very seriously."

Kel laughed. "Secret societies? Like the Freemasons or something?"

"Exactly," Rod said, leaning in conspiratorially. "He used to joke that the league was more than just a golf club. Said we had a higher purpose, something to do with... enlightenment." He winked.

Kel's interest was piqued. "Enlightenment, huh? Sounds deep for a golf league."

"Oh, you'd be surprised," Rod said, swinging his club again. "He had us doing these strange little rituals before every round. Like tapping our clubs three times on the ground before a drive. Said it was to honor the 'keepers of the course.'"

Kel laughed again. "Keepers of the course? That sounds like something out of a fantasy novel."

Rod grinned. "Yeah, it does. But Larry was dead serious. Even had this old leather-bound book full of strange symbols and chants. Said it was passed down from his grandfather, who was a railroad engineer and a Freemason. Larry believed we were all part of some grand tradition.

Larry Carlisle's Secret Book

Kel raised an eyebrow. "Are you saying Larry thought we were part of the Illuminati or something?"

Rod shrugged. "Who knows? He did like to call our championship trophy the 'Illuminated Cup.' Some of us thought it was just a joke. But every now and then, he'd look at you with those piercing eyes, and you'd wonder if he knew something we didn't."

"Sounds like Larry was quite the storyteller," Kel said, shaking his head with a smile.

Rod sighed nostalgically. "Oh, he was. But you know, sometimes I think there was more to it, like how the clubhouse always gets struck by lightning on the same day every year. Or the way the grass on the 18th hole always seems greener than anywhere else on the course. Little things like that. Even the course name is kind of strange, The Mythos, don't ya think?"

Kel smiled. "You're making this sound more and more mysterious, Rod."

Rod gave a knowing smile. "Just keep your eyes open, Kel. The Grand Trunk Golf League has its secrets. And who knows, maybe one day you'll find out just how deep they go.

As the evening progressed, stories of the round were shared, accompanied by laughter and good-natured ribbing. In the end, it wasn't just about who hit the longest drives or sunk the most putts. It was about the joy of playing golf, the bonds formed through friendly competition, and the camaraderie shared among the members of the Grand Trunk Golf League.

The Grand Trunk Golf League, established fifty years ago, was the brainchild of two enigmatic union railroad workers, Larry Carlisle and Steve Grillo. Both men, deeply involved with the Grand Trunk Western Railroad Company in the 1970s, shared more than just a passion for golf—they were rumored to be part of a secret society that traced its roots back to the ancient order of the Illuminati. The Grand Trunk Western itself emerged from a collection of about fifteen 19th-century Michigan rail lines, such as the Chicago and Grand Trunk Railway and the Detroit and Huron Railway, each with its own storied history. At 82 years of age, Larry was the sole living founding member of the league.

Larry Carlisle circa 1970's

Carlisle and Grillo, inspired by the clandestine traditions and symbols of their society, envisioned the golf league as not just a recreational activity but a continuation of their esoteric heritage. Hidden within the league's seemingly ordinary traditions were rituals and codes that only the initiated could fully understand, blending the camaraderie of the railway workers with the mystique of ancient secrets.

However, over the decades, the true nature of the league's origins became a subject of playful debate among its members. Many newer members, hearing tales of Illuminati connections and secret rituals, were left uncertain whether these stories were historical facts or elaborate jokes. The mystique was further fueled by the fact that not every member could recall attending their many separate weekend golf outings at various Michigan courses like The Vision and The Dread. This ambiguity only added to the charm and allure of the league, leaving each member to decide for themselves where the line between reality and fiction lay.

As the evening progressed, stories of the round were shared, accompanied by laughter and good-natured ribbing. It wasn't just about who hit the longest drives or sunk the most putts. It was about the joy of playing golf, the bonds formed through friendly competition, and the camaraderie shared among the members of the Grand Trunk Golf League. As they reminisced about their many outings, the names of courses the golf league members frequented came up – Arcadia Links, with its serene, almost dreamlike quality, and Shadowmoor, a course that tested even the bravest with its eerie foreboding design. These names, much like Mythos, added to the allure and mystery that had become the hallmark of the Grand Trunk Golf League.

Kelvin found himself reflecting on his conversation with Rod and the peculiarities he'd noticed throughout the day. The cryptic engraving on Tony's putter, the strange tapping ritual, and Ron's odd phrases during his drives all pointed to something more than mere superstition. Maybe there was some truth to the stories about the league's mysterious origins.

As they settled into their seats at PJ's Pub, Kel couldn't help but feel a sense of belonging. Despite the age gap and the league's peculiar traditions, he felt a connection to these men and their shared history. Raising his glass in a toast, he said, "To the Grand Trunk Golf League and to many more rounds filled with friendship and mystery."

The others raised their glasses in response, their eyes twinkling with the same blend of humor and camaraderie. Ron, still reveling in his role as "The Dicktator," smirked. "Here's to keeping the tradition alive, even if it's a bit... Illuminated."

Tony chimed in, "In unity and precision, we find the cup, right?"

Kel laughed, "Exactly. Who knows, maybe one day I'll get to hold that Illuminated Cup myself."

Randy smiled warmly. "Just remember, Kel, it's not always about what you see. Sometimes, it's about what you feel and the stories you become a part of."

Remaining retired GT Railroad workers still in GT Golf League 2023

As they clinked their beer bottles and mixed drink glasses, Kelvin felt a sense of purpose. He wasn't just playing golf; he was becoming part of a legacy, one filled with stories, secrets, and a sense of wonder. Whether or not the tales of the Illuminati were true, he knew he had found something special.

The Grand Trunk Golf League, with its blend of camaraderie and mystery, was more than just a league. It was a living, breathing tradition, a tapestry woven with the threads of history, friendship, and, perhaps, a touch of the extraordinary.

Kelvin left PJ's Pub that night with a smile on his face, feeling as if he had found his place among these storied greens and fairways. The league's secrets might unravel over time, or they might remain an intriguing mystery. Either way, Kelvin knew he was exactly where he was meant to be—right in the heart of the Grand Trunk Golf League.

Chapter 5:
Bowhunting Banter: A Tale of Machismo and Mockery

Iron Workers Local 22 is located in Indianapolis, IN, with regional offices in Terre Haute and Lafayette. The local has always served a diverse area to meet the needs of its members and contractors. As a local with over 1,000 members, they offer some great training and technology to help advance the construction industry. Their apprenticeship program is designed to ensure its members are highly skilled and qualified to be as productive as possible. At times, it seemed that the main member qualifications were a penchant for drinking, a prior criminal record, and an interest in hunting and fishing.

Donny Wallen, Tom Randall, Jonny Randall, and Jim Nether (also known as "Bonehead") all met in Iron Workers apprentice school and worked several iron jobs together over the years. To become an Iron Worker, one must attend technical training via Apprentice school. While attending said school, they then apply those skills on the job over several years until one achieves a mastery level called Journeyman. Pay increases significantly from Apprentice to Journeyman status. All four men had achieved Journeyman status as Iron Workers, both from formal school and the school of Hard Knocks. Donny got a criminal record shortly after high school when he punched a local sheriff. Bonehead did 90 days in the Martinsville Jail following his third DUI. Brothers Tom and Jonny had collectively earned some time on assault charges following a brilliant barroom brawl in Pat's Tavern in Mooresville, IN. They all had calmed over the years and spent their free time more productively with archery and deer hunting. Donny bought some land just outside of Mooresville, IN, and had arranged a respecable archery range. One fall day, not too long ago, the friends congregated at Donny's self-made archery range.

Donny's Archery Range is a serene woodland setting near Centerton, IN, nestled within the heart of South-Central Indiana's rolling hills and dense forests. Towering oak and maple trees create a natural canopy that filters the golden sunlight, casting dappled shadows on the forest floor. The crisp scent of fallen leaves and damp earth mingles with the faint aroma of wood smoke, giving the air an earthy, comforting quality.

Scattered throughout the woodland are lifelike 3D animal targets strategically placed among the trees. Donny, with a keen eye for detail, sets up a wild boar target about 20 yards away from his station. He carefully positions it next to a massive oak, its sturdy branches providing a striking backdrop to the target. Nearby, a turkey target is nestled between two indigenous bushes, their leaves rustling in the gentle breeze. Donny's appreciation for the natural beauty extends to the surrounding bushes. He notes the presence of Viburnums, including Southern arrowwoodblack haw and nannyberry, their delicate blossoms adding a touch of elegance to the woodland.

Donny Wallen

Witchhazel, with its distinctive spidery blossoms, graces the landscape, adding a splash of color to the forest floor. Donny spots a common witch hazel nearby, standing tall at 15-20 feet, its branches reaching out in all directions. Oakleaf hydrangea, a testament to the diversity of plant life, adorns the underbrush, its white, cone-shaped flowers standing out against the vibrant green leaves. Grey dogwood and black chokeberry complete the ensemble, their clusters of white blossoms and dark berries contributing to the rich tapestry of flora.

Bonehead: (flexing his muscles) Ah, Donny, my trusty comrade! Today, we shall shoot arrows like warriors using our handmade recurve bows!

Donny: (rolling his eyes) Bonehead, when will you realize that draw weight isn't everything? It's about skill and precision, my friend. And look at my fletched wooden arrows, pure craftsmanship!

Tom: (adjusting his compound bow) Hey, Bonehead, I see you're still struggling with that brute force of yours. Why don't you join the modern age and get yourself a compound bow like me? These babies make hitting targets a breeze!

Bonehead: (gritting his teeth) Compound bows, Tom? You compounders are just a bunch of "button-sucking wheel heads"? Anyone can pull a mechanical bow, kiss the button on the string, and hit a target. real men use the recurve!

Jonny: (smirking) Hey, Bonehead, at least Tom can hit the target with that fancy compound bow. He doesn't need to strain every muscle just to draw his bow. And look at my scope! No need to guess where my arrow's going, my friend.

Tom Randall

Donny: (chuckles) Well said, Jonny. We've all come a long way from those rowdy days at the local. This brotherhood means more than just iron and arrows.

Bonehead: You know, Donny, this massive bow of mine, it's handmade by a fellow named Fred Bear. World-renowned archer, you know. Donny and I here, we're big fans of the late Fred Bear.

Tom: (nodding) That's right, Bonehead. Fred Bear was quite the legend. First president of Michigan's oldest archery club, Detroit Archers. He left a mark on the world of archery that'll last forever.

Jonny: And let's not forget, Ted Nugent, , he appreciated Fred Bear, too. He kinda immortalized Fred in the song "Fred Bear" in that Spirit of the Wild album he put out. Ted Nugent was Bear's friend, you know.

Donny: (grinning) But Bonehead, for all his skill and fame, Fred Bear never hunted with one of those gadget-infested compound bows. He kept it pure and simple, just like we do.

Bonehead: (smirking) Well, Donny, maybe he'd change his tune if he tried one of these bad boys. There's a reason technology advances, you know.

Jonny: (turning to Donny) Hey Donny, how's your oldest boy doing up in Michigan? Still working for General Motors?

Donny: (smiling) Oh, he's doing well, Jonny. Living up in Detroit, working hard at General Motors. Making us proud. He had a brush with greatness one time, you know. Met Fred Bear at an archery event.

Jonny: (intrigued) No kidding! What was Fred Bear like?

Donny: (reflecting) I never had the pleasure of meeting him myself, but from what my boy tells me, Fred Bear was a down-to-earth man. Hardworking, just like the rest of us. Early on, Bear worked as a glue maker for the Chrysler Company in Detroit. He also worked for the Ford Motor Company in Detroit as a wood carver, making cabinets for the radios and dashboards.

Bonehead: (nodding) Now that's something. A man of many talents, old Fred Bear.

Donny: (proudly) Absolutely. He made his mark in the world of archery and never forgot his roots.

Tom: (playfully) Bonehead, I reckon the forest will echo with three sounds: the snap of your rotator cuff, a yelp that'd put a schoolgirl to shame, and the buck high-tailing it out of there!

Bonehead: (laughing) Well, Tom, let's see you do better with that fancy contraption of yours!

As Bonehead, Donny, Tom, and Jonny continue to practice their archery, the camaraderie and banter flow as naturally as the gentle breeze through the forest. Each arrow released is a testament to their shared passion for the sport and the unbreakable bonds forged through years of friendship.

Bonehead

And so, my friends, let's raise our bows and toast to these characters, their machismo, and their hilariously competitive spirit. May they hit their targets, even if it takes a little friendly teasing to get there. Let's raise a beer to Fred Bear, an archery pioneer whose ashes are spread near his favorite fly-fishing spot along the Au Sable River in Northern Lower Michigan. Let's thank Ted Nugent for immortalizing Fred in his songs. RIP, Fred Bear. Let's also thank Bass Pro Shops for its maintenance of the Fred Bear Museum collections, which originated in Grayling, MI.

Fred and Ted

Chapter 6:
Machismo Glow: – The Battle of Festive Titans

Jimmy Jackson has been a news reporter for the Oakland County Press for over 20 years. Over the past decade or so, he earned the nickname "Jimmy Jingle" for his fabulous and nearly decade-long coverage of four gentlemen he befriended on Wright Street in Woodstock, Michigan. The relationship and news coverage evolved from a simple story about Christmas spirit and home decorating fanatics to statewide coverage, evolving Woodstock from a small, quiet Detroit suburb to an indelible mark on the Michigan holiday map. Jimmy's coverage in the Oakland County Press was picked up by the Detroit Free Press and several other state news reports shortly following his larger-than-life depictions of the Christmas Quartet in action and characterizations of Big Hank the Hammer, Tinsmith Tony, Marcus "The Maverick" and Carlos "The Craftsmen" and the subsequent naming of their artistic displays. His series of weekly stories created buzz and excitement and drove many Michiganders to Woodstock for a holiday tour down Wright Street. This year, Jimmy is supplementing his regular printed articles with a new live-action reporting approach, capturing live coverage, and posting on the Oakland County Press's newly created Substack podcast as well as its' other social mediums.

Jimmy "The Jingle" Jackson circa 2019

The Legendary Quartet:

Back in Woodstock, the decoration process had commenced on the weekend prior to Thanksgiving. Like standard work, Jimmy was making his rounds with the Fab Four talking strategy. His first stop was with Hank the Hammer. Camera crew in tow, Jimmy approaches the driveway of Hank Henderson, where Hank, foreknowing his arrival time, walks away from his work toward Jimmy. Jimmy, sporting a rugged style in a leather jacket adorned with holiday-themed patches and a Stormy Kromer cap, moves with a confident swagger, exuding an air of self-assuredness. His steps are purposeful, and his erect posture reflects an almost theatrical manly demeanor.

With a deep and resonant voice carrying a hint of gravel, Jimmy shouts, "Hey Hammer, my man, ready to do this thing?"

Big Hank, a towering figure, former lumberjack, and Marine Corps veteran from the Upper Peninsula, reached out his hand to Jimmy, shaking it heartily, and in a deep booming voice that resonated with the confidence of a seasoned commander, exclaimed, "Let's get it on."

Looking at the camera and seeing the red record light illuminated, Jimmy raises his microphone. "I am here live in Woodstock with the Commander of Luminescence, creator of The Luminary Lodge concept, none other than Hank "The Hammer Henderson." Hello again, Hank, great to see you again, my friend, so what do you have in store for us this year?"

Hank looks toward the camera and booms, "Well, Jimmy, as you can see there in the front yard, me and the Misses intend to keep with the lodge concept using our log cabin replica, LED tree lights and chainsaw carved ornamentals. But we are going to pump it up a bit with some top-secret upgrades."

"Holy Cow, top secret upgrades. Can you let us in on that a bit Hammer"?

"Well, Jimmy, don't want to give up too much on that. You know we got some friendly competition over there with Tony Tinsmith, Maverick, and Carlos." What I can say, though, is expect some smoke, several new chainsaw carvings, and, uh, let's say, towering sentinels.

"That sounds fabulous, Hank. Well, folks, you heard it here first. The Commander of Luminesce is gonna' carve it up lumberjack style, says where there is smoke, there's fire and maybe a towering inferno of luminescence. This is Jimmy "The Jingle" Jackson, Oakland County Press, live from Woodstock."

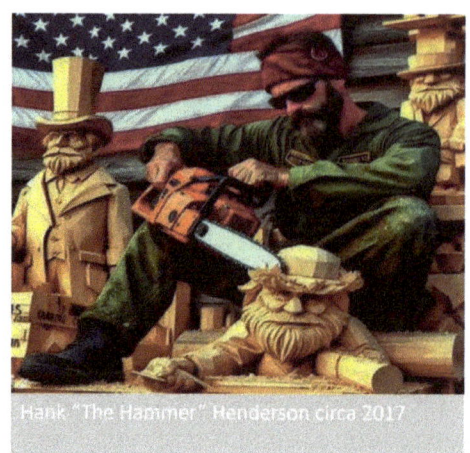
Hank "The Hammer" Henderson circa 2017

In the background, like clockwork, the remainder of the Fab Four gazed in appreciation, yet partly smiling, having scene Jimmy's sports commentator style. Jimmy looked over toward them, nodded and inquired. "Good morning, gentlemen. You guys ready to roll? Thought Tony might want to go next, then you Maverick and Carlos last – in-house run order?"

Tony nodded and said, "Right On, JJ." Maverick and Carlos responded with thumbs up.

In Tony's front yard, the camera rolled. "Hello Michigan, Jimmy the Jingle here live again in Woodstock at the home of Tony Rodriguez. Better known to you as "The Tinsmith" and the famous work he calls "Electric Elegance." My, what a display these past few years, Tony. Do you intend to continue with your symphony of synchronized lights and those handcrafted metal ornaments? I know many of the ladies loved your nutcrackers last year." Jimmy finished his opener with a wink and tongue-in-cheek grin toward the camera and repeated the expressions to Tony.

Tony nods and, with a pressed smile, holds back a laugh from the nutcracker comment, simultaneously appreciating Jimmy's bravado. He walks toward the camera with a sort of tech-savvy swagger as if he were the James Bond of holiday gadgets. Tony explains in James Bond's bravado tech-savvy style. "Our display, Electric Elegance, has always centered around the cross-section of where holiday spirit meets virtual reality. We turn ordinary decorations into freakin' technological marvels, you know, Jimmy, like where gadgets come to life."

"Well, Tony, you are the Gadget Maestro, the Sultan of Holiday Techno. What futuristic features will you unleash for us this year?" Requested Jimmy.

"As Hank noted earlier, Jimmy, I don't want to divulge too much, but let me say this. As with the tradition of "Electric Elegance," expect to see some of our similar synchronized twinkling lights choreographed to famous holiday tunes. And of course, I will keep the ladies pleased with my handcrafted metal nutcrackers," Tony explains with crossed arms and nods and pressed grin and then continues. "But you will see what my lovely wife calls *The piece de resistance*," Tony says in his attempted French accent. "Think life-sized, think animatronic, think AI and integration."

Jimmy's eyes widened and he could hardly get the next words out. He was captured by the machismo moment as he closed on this piece of the live interview. "Well, that's giving me some holiday iron, just thinking about it. Incredible, rocking out to tunes, technology and animatronics. And bringing in a special piece that no one can resist. This is Jimmy the Jingle live again, Oakland County Press, here in Woodstock."

With the camera off now, Jimmy looked to Hank and Tony, who approved with nods and grins, barely containing themselves having heard Jimmy's machismo banter with a sexual undertone. He looked across the street to Maverick and Carlos. "Hey Marcus, coming to you next."

Tony "The Tinsmith" Rodriguez in his workshop circa 2020 developing the "Ice Gear Snowflake"

Jimmy swaggered across Wright Street to Marcus's yard, cameraman in tow; he raised his microphone and began. "Jimmy Jingle live here with Marcus Monroe in Woodstock. Marcus is known to many of you as a founding member of what I coined as "The Fab Four," the Legendary Holiday Quartet and creator of Frosty's Fury. Marcus, what do you have in the works this year?"

"Yeah, Jimmy, well, you know we like to build on our strengths here. My kids and wife like to think we are like snow-sculpting mavericks". Marcus explains like a cowboy stuntman, laid back, arms crossed, rocking back and forth on his leather work boots as he speaks. He continues. "Expect to see the ice rink-our signature; expect to see our patented snow sculptures made rock hard – Marcus says as he curls his right arm up in front of his face, hand in fist and flexing his bicep; he pumps his waste forward in choreographed fashion. I like to have our snow sculptures reflect some of our extreme sports of snowboarding and snow mountain biking and of course, our passion for hockey. What you will see this year is a definitive theme unlike any before, sporting daring and innovative sculptures, like an icy daring wonderland. There will be something new, let's say, something daring and sloppy."

Jimmy chimes in with the microphone, accelerating the machismo banter laced with a more sexual undertone. "Thank you, Marcus, always a pleasure seeing your rock-hard sculpture. So glad you will continue with the ice rink, a crowd favorite. Now let's see what kind of curvy, slopy fury goodness you have in store for us". Live again here in Woodstock with Marcus "The Maverick" Monroe and the evolution of Frosty's Fury."

As the camera dropped and the light extinguished, Jimmy and Marcus looked each other in the eye and belted a few hearty laughs, both a little full of themselves from their performance. "Right on!" exclaimed Marcus as the two joined in waist-high fist pumps. Hank, Tony, and Carlos smirky-smiled and collectively nodded in approval.

Marcus "The Maverick" Monroe with patented ice carving process circa 2020

Without another word, Jimmy and the cameraman strolled next door to Carlos' home. Carlos is in the lead. And, like automation, proceeded with the final interview.

"Jimmy, The Jingle Jackson here, live in Woodstock, I am speaking with Carlos "The Craftsman" Castillo, creator of the

Celestial Citadel. Hello Carlos. We are anxiously awaiting the unveil of this year's celestial magic. Give us some insight, please."

"You know the neighbors refer to me as the somewhat artisan of our so-called quartet. I appreciate old world tradition, and you can say that my hands are, uhm, maybe guided by uhm, like holiday magic. Every ornament I create tells a tale; every glimmering light is like poetry."

Carlos then looks straight into the camera, canting his head down and to the right and raising and opening his hands in front of his chin and with a closed mouth smile says. "My magic lies in the quiet resilience of an artisan's touch, so my wife says. You can expect some real magic this year, Jimmy. I will continue with my intricate wooden angels, adding in several celestial beings, let's say, each with a different instrument. I am going for a sort of heavenly orchestra vibe. This year, we will add in a light show, it will mimic something celestial you all know and love that will bathe the entire neighborhood in a mesmerizing glow."

Jimmy then pulls back the microphone from Carlos. "That almost sounds erotic, Carlos. Makes me hot with excitement. Wow, folks, The Celestial Citadel will be bringing some otherworldly magic to Woodstock. En Fuego! Stay tuned, Michiganders, for future coverage as the Fab Four, the Holiday Quartet, bring it to Woodstock. Again, this is Jimmy the Jingle Jackson, live on Wright Street in beautiful Woodstock.

Jimmy's Epiphany:

During the prior Christmas holiday, Jimmy had an epiphany at the Oakland County Press annual Christmas party, which he shared with the Fab Four

Jimmy "The Jingle" Jackson, with his swagger as bold as a yuletide trumpet, recognized the need to rouse the town from its seasonal slumber in the forthcoming year. The idea of a contest, a machismo showdown, simmered in Jimmy's mind like a pot of spiced cider ready to be poured. The idea was to have a judging process, with criteria, grading etc., culminating in an award ceremony. Jimmy and the Fab Four identified various award criteria and developed a survey for the communities to decide. A process to include new entrants. A brilliant idea. One that is revolutionary and would most likely propel Jimmy, the Fab Four and Woodstock to national stardom. Jimmy had full backing from the establishment. Send out the survey before Christmas, have the people pick the winners, and then have a televised award ceremony at the Oakland County Press Christmas party.

The Oakland Country press and Jimmy were now very busy in the following weeks executing their plan and promoting the contest through their Substack newsletter and podcast, their social media sites and Jimmy's normal arterial assault array of weekly articles in the Oakland County Press's Sunday morning printed publication.

Maxwell Frost's Arrival:

On a whim, Maxwell Frost took a coast-to-coast flight layover opportunity to visit Detroit. In a cozy Detroit bookstore, he, captivated by the melodies of Christmas carols playing softly in the background, caught wind of Jimmy's spirited announcement. Michigan's energy vibrated through the frost-kissed windowpanes.

As he perused the holiday-themed section, a spirited conversation reached his ears. "Did you hear Jimmy the Jingle announcing a contest? A statewide showdown right here in the Detroit suburbs!" exclaimed a passionate reader to their companion.

Maxwell Frost, the wandering wordsmith of the holiday spirit, is a figure of distinct character and charm. His appearance is a mix of timeless elegance and a hint of quirky charm that befits a man who has traversed the globe in search of the most festive stories. Maxwell was famous for his reporting of notable Christmas light competitions and displays. His resume being unprecedented. He single-handedly found and exposed *Dyker Heights* in Brooklyn, New York bringing visitors from all over the world. He then exposed the West Coast through his coverage of the *Thoroughbred Christmas Lights* in Rancho Cucamonga, CA. He expanded his portfolio globally with the *Christmas Festival of Lights* in Melbourne and the *Festival of Lights* at VanDusen Botanical Gardens in Vancouver, Canada. Maxwell's work fostered the creation and annual publication of the *Global Glitter Gala*, a quarterly publication that offers unique and festive articles and holiday goods advertising. In the past several years, the spirit of

Christmas has seemed to wane from his perspective. Maxwell longs for a way to revive it.

Maxwell stands at a moderate height; his frame is lean and wiry, a testament to the countless miles he's walked in pursuit of tales from every corner of the world. His hair was full, shoulder length and wavy, a shade somewhere between salt and pepper, is meticulously groomed and styled in a way that suggests both sophistication and a touch of untamed spirit. His thick but well trimmed beard added to his blended rustic appearance.

His eyes are the kind that has seen the flickering glow of countless candles and twinkling lights. Behind his wire-framed glasses, those eyes sparkle with a warmth that reflects the joy he's witnessed in every Christmas celebration. There's a keen intelligence in his gaze, a storyteller's insight that has been honed by years of capturing the magic of the holiday season.

Maxwell's wardrobe is a delightful fusion of classic and whimsical. On any given day, he might be found in a well-tailored tweed coat adorned with an array of festive enamel pins, each representing a different Christmas market or celebration he's covered. His scarves are a vibrant tapestry of colors, as if he's woven the spirit of various holiday traditions into the fabric.

A perpetually worn leather satchel, battered but well cared for, hangs casually over his shoulder. It contains the tools of his trade – which today is a mobile phone and laptop that begrudgingly replaced his vintage camera and a dog-eared notebook filled with handwritten anecdotes. However, he still maintains a small collection of quirky ornaments gathered from the corners of the Earth.

Maxwell's attire is completed by a pair of very sturdy yet stylish boots, well-worn from countless journeys. There's a jauntiness in his step, a rhythm that echoes the festive melodies he's encountered in Christmas markets from Vienna to Tokyo.

In essence, Maxwell Frost is a timeless figure with a touch of whimsy, a man whose appearance mirrors the kaleidoscope of cultures and celebrations he's woven into the fabric of his festive tales.

Maxwell, intrigued by the prospect of a machismo-laden holiday spectacle, leaned in to catch more snippets of the conversation. The idea of a festive clash and the mention of the quartet's prowess in decoration captured his adventurous spirit.

Maxwell thought to himself, "A contest, a quartet of titans, you have piqued my curiosity. Woodstock, you've just earned a spot on my holiday itinerary. This is just the kind of thing that will put spark back in Christmas." Maxwell was befuddled at how he had missed Detroit in his travels and the quirky publications of Jimmy "The Jingle." Maybe some spirit of Christmas intervention had set him on this path to The Motor City.

Maxwell Frost. Detroit circa 2021

Scene 4: The Global Glitter Gala Unveiled:

Maxwell, inspired by the quartet's machismo spirit, decides to elevate the contest to a global level. He contacts Jimmy through the Oakland County Press and schedules a meeting with Jimmy in a café in Rochester where he recalls the festivity and annual display of lights on the businesses in downtown Rochester. Jimmy encourages Maxwell to review his prior publications and Substack podcast prior to their meeting. There, he talks to Jimmy about his ideas for what he calls the *Global Glitter Gala*, a competition that will put Woodstock on the map. And how many potential sponsors might join the festive fray. He plans to announce this in his upcoming quarterly editorial at the *Global Glitter Gala*. But he has one major piece of professional advice for Jimmy's quirky machismo communication style.

As Jimmy intently listens to Maxwell, his inner dialogue is firing: "This could really put Woodstock on the map. And make the Fab Four truly fabulous. And all the stories I could publish at new levels. Me, Jimmy 'The Jingle", on the global stage."

Maxwell softens his voice as he speaks across the café table. "Jimmy, thank you for directing me to your prior works and especially the podcast. I really appreciate your machismo-laced enthusiasm and interactions with your pals there. I love the nicknames and the naming of their displays which you coined over several years. However, with all due respect, I think you need to drop the sexual undertones. Don't get me wrong, I love being manly, joking with my boys and all, lots of fun banter. I just don't think it has a place with the public message of Christmas. That kind of talk is best shared between buddies. Frankly speaking, I do not think we will pull this Gala extravaganza off if you continue in public settings with that tone of discourse. "

Jimmy bows his head, and looking down at the table, takes to heart Maxwell's sincere advice and feels shame. Rethinking his behavior, he says to Maxwell. "You are right, Maxwell. That did get a bit out of hand. I agree. Like you, I want to bring back that Christmas buzz that has seemed to have waned over the past several years. We don't need to sexualize Christmas. Let me talk to the crew. Let 'em know we need to tame our public discourse. Probably best if I edit out those raunchy one-liners on the podcast and repost it." "Great idea, Jimmy. I appreciate your consideration." Says Maxwell with a smile on his face and a twinkle in his eye.

Decorating War:

The quartet, now aware of the global spotlight, engages in a decorating war fueled by machismo banter and competitive spirit. Jimmy's tough love and Maxwell's smooth encouragement push the quartet to new heights as the town transforms into a holiday battleground. Several other neighbors in Woodstock have started their own displays. Attics are emptied, store shelves are nearing bare as the folks from cities all over Michigan and the United States learn of the regional, state, and global competition. Christmas ornaments, nativities, and lights of all kinds are in short supply. Seems as though everyone wants in on the action. The scene is similar across the globe, from time zone to time zone, everywhere that Christmas is celebrated.

As the quartet works feverishly in their yards, you can hear hammers pounding, chainsaws carving, animatronic motors whirling and the conversations of the Fab Four.

Big Hank to Tony: "I am amazed what Jimmy has pulled off here, taking this thing global. Makes me really want to step up my game. Can you believe that the owner of my company told me to take off all the time I needed to pull this off"?

Tony shouts back: "So cool of them. Amazing how the town and businesses are all coming together on this. Joe down at the hardware store offered up any metal I need. And my supervisor said I could use any equipment I needed from our machine shop".

Marcus is talking to Carlos in Carlos's front yard: "Have you been downtown this past week and seen all the older homes in the historic section? Looks like they drained the shelves at half the hardware stores in the county. Lights, like every blow-up figure imaginable out there. They are stepping up their game."

Carlos replies, "Pretty awesome stuff. So happy to see this. But they have a long way to go to rival your art, Marcus. You are really pulling in the teenage crowd. I saw a bunch of kids making some awesome jumps at the ski hill. They are taking your lead, building figures and faces into the snow jumps and berms they have built over there."

The Global Gala Unleashed:

The night of the Global Glitter Gala arrives. Woodstock is the epicenter and launching point of the global contest. The quartet's machismo displays are broadcast to the world, captivating audiences with their creativity, originality, and macho flair. Maxwell and Jimmy, with their distinct styles, co-host the event, adding a touch of festive yet clean-natured machismo to the global celebration. As they walk from display to display, filmed by local, national, and global crews, they are followed by a huge crowd. Jimmy and Maxwell speak to the Fab Four displays and global crowds as if they were announcers in the first round of *March Madness* or the *World Cup*.

As Maxwell Frost wanders down Wright Street, the epicenter of the machismo Christmas displays, he can't help but feel a unique energy pulsating through the air. The quartet's displays, with their machismo flair, strike a chord with Maxwell that transcends the ordinary festivity he has encountered in his global travels. As he observes each house, he is genuinely moved, and a range of emotions begins to stir within him.

Jimmy: "Hello Michigan. Jimmy The Jingle Jackson representing the Oakland County Press here with the legendary Maxwell Frost coming to you live from Woodstock, Michigan. We are bringing to you the first ever *Global Glitter Gala*, a global Christmas decoration extravaganza".

Maxwell: "So true, Jimmy, an extravaganza. I would like to thank the *Global Glitter Gala* magazine and Oakland County Press as the originators of this great event. I am so pleased to be here, to see this fabulous display of Christmas spirit. You know Jimmy, I have traveled the world seeking and reporting on festivity, I have just never been part of anything like this, a regional and state playoff, which moves to a national semifinal, culminating in a global championship. This is the opportunity we have created and call The Global Glitter Gala. With that, Jimmy, let's take our tour, shall we?"

Jimmy: "Folks, here we have the Luminary Lodge and creator Hank "The Hammer" Henderson. What a massive light display he has here, Maxwell. Just look how he has adorned his home and trees with what I would call just a colossal display of LED lights. The giant oak and maple trees towering like sentinels guarding the property."

Maxwell gazes at Hank's Luminary Lodge, with its colossal LED light trees and chainsaw-carved ornaments depicting classic Christmas stories.

Maxwell: (inwardly) What an extraordinary amalgamation of rugged charm and festive storytelling. This Luminary Lodge captures the essence of Christmas tales in a way I've rarely witnessed. The dedication to detail and the towering LED sentinels create a spectacle that tugs at the heartstrings. This inward monologue continues with Maxwell as he sees the other displays and continues his reporting with Jimmy.

Maxwell: "I thoroughly relish the rugged charm of the chainsaw-carved ornaments which so eloquently depict all these fabulous Christmas stories. I love how he has captured the essence of Ebenezer Scrooge, Tiny Tim, and the Ghosts of Christmas Past, Present, and Future, literally bringing to life Dickens' timeless tale of redemption and generosity before our very eyes.

Jimmy: "And let us not forget the signature log cabin replica. And just amazing how they have a working chimney puffing away there. Just a classic piece of work."

Maxwell: "Let us move along to Electric Elegance?" Jimmy nods in agreement.

Jimmy: "Take it away, Maxwell."

Maxwell: "I understand that Tony "The Tinsmith" Rodriguez is the architect of this symphony of synchronized lights. All the intricately woven lights keeping beat to the sound of various holiday music emanating from a soothing sound system. Those intricate patterns and twinkling bulbs are like a choreographed dance unfolding before us. And Jimmy, I think you mentioned that Tony handcrafts those dazzlingly bright metal ornaments in his workshop here on location"?

Jimmy: "Yes, Maxwell. Tony is a machinist in his day job. Just a fabulous knack for precision. Look at the detail in the shimmering snowflakes and those polished metal nutcrackers of various designs."

Maxwell: "And, of course, I would be remiss to not mention the life-sized animatronics. I see there is Santa waving at us, and then his reindeer crew appear to be snacking on the lawn as if they are a heard in the wild. And the elf workshop, looks like a real action workshop. Those elves are truly building toys as we watch. Amazing technology!"

Jimmy: "Well, across the street here, Maxwell, let's take a stroll and visit "Frosty's Fury" and creator Marcus 'The Maverick Monroe." You know Marcus and his family are quite the thrill seekers. Hockey players, snowboarders and mountain bike riders. And they have really incorporated this passion into their display. The ice rink has always been a staple in Maverick's designs and used most every weekend by friends, family, and neighbors. They even constructed a miniature Zamboni to polish the ice. So well-lit from under the ice, and almost painstaking detail in the under-ice lighting and graphics."

Maxwell: "And the centerpiece this year is that daring sledding slope, with LED-lit ice-carved snowboarders racing down it. And their own snow machine is keeping it cold. It is like we stepped into Colorado just walking down the street. Truly amazing!"

Jimmy: "And lastly, on our tour of Wright Street is the Celestial Citadel created by Carlos "The Craftsmen" Castillo. Maxwell, he has literally transformed his property into a celestial kingdom with the hanging stars and planets suspended from the rustic oak and pines in the yard".

Maxwell: "Carlos mentioned to me that he handcrafts those intricate wooden angels and now I see that he has enhanced that design as each is holding its own unique instrument. One might say that is a heavenly orchestra."

Jimmy: "Just like Heaven, Maxwell and with a touch of magic, too. The light show he has enabled is mimicking the Northern Lights. Imagine that, right here in Woodstock, we can see his rendition of the Northern Lights."

Maxwell: "It is most certainly a mesmerizing glow" I truly believe that he has truly transcended traditional Christmas themes with this almost avant-garde, innovative, and boundary-pushing display. "

The night continued as Maxwell and Jimmy toured the town of Woodstock, reporting on all types of submissions and displays. But Wright Street was the epicenter, and nothing in town, or the state for that matter, matched up the magnificence of the Wright Street Quartet, The Fab Four.

Winners and Revelations:

At the Oakland County Press global Christmas party, the results of the Global contest were unveiled. As the winners are announced—Big Hank, Tony "The Tinsmith," Marcus "The Maverick," and Carlos "The Craftsman"—the quartet learns of the global impact of their machismo displays. Maxwell and Jimmy share a festive toast, realizing that the machismo glow of Woodstock has left an indelible mark on the holiday map. With the help of the Global Glitter Gala staff and other interests globally, the first-ever holiday decoration and reward schema was introduced. The Fab Four displays were a great influence on the Award Scheme.

Best Overall Display - The Grand Luminary Trophy:

Winner: Hank "The Hammer" Henderson for Luminary Lodge.

Justification: Hank's colossal LED light trees, chainsaw-carved ornaments, and the log cabin replica captured the essence of

Christmas tales and showcased a perfect blend of creativity, tradition, and innovation.

Innovative Techno Marvel - The Electric Elegance Accolade:

Winner: Tony "The Tinsmith" Rodriguez for Electric Elegance.

Justification: Tony's synchronized lights, handcrafted metal ornaments, and life-sized animatronics demonstrated exceptional technological prowess, creating a unique and dazzling holiday spectacle.

Thrilling Winter Wonderland - Frosty's Fury Triumph Trophy
Winner: Marcus "The Maverick" Monroe for Frosty's Fury.

Justification: Marcus's incorporation of winter sports themes, the ice rink, daring sculptures, and the towering sledding slope brought an adventurous and thrilling edge to the Christmas displays.

Celestial Artistry - The Celestial Citadel Crown:

Winner: Carlos "The Craftsman" Castillo for Celestial Citadel.

Justification: Carlos's intricate wooden angels, celestial beings, and the mesmerizing light show created a celestial kingdom, showcasing artistry and a touch of magic.

As the town had come alive with Christmas spirit, Jimmy and Maxwell felt the need to create additional awards. These additional awards recognize the diverse contributions and efforts of participants beyond the quartet, celebrating creativity, community engagement, sustainability, and the heartfelt essence of the holiday season.

Best Newcomer - Rising Star Ornament:

Winner: A late entrant, Leroy Tate and Pat Thompson, for their charming and creative display that added a fresh touch to the Woodstock tradition.

Community Spirit Award - Unity Wreath:

Winner: The Johnson Family for their collaborative neighborhood display that brought together various elements, fostering a sense of community spirit.

Eco-Friendly Innovator - Green Globe Trophy:

Winner: The Smiths for their display that utilized sustainable materials and energy-efficient lighting, promoting an environmentally conscious approach.

Most Heartwarming - Love & Lights Plaque:

Winner: Mrs. Jenkins, an elderly resident, for her simple yet heartwarming display that radiated the true spirit of Christmas and touched the community's hearts. With special accolades for the great support from Woodstock Boy Scout Troop 728.

Epilogue:

Woodstock becomes a holiday destination, attracting visitors from around the world. The quartet's machismo legacy lives on, and the Global Glitter Gala becomes an annual tradition, thanks to the charismatic duo of Jimmy "The Jingle" Jackson and Maxwell Frost, who, with a touch of machismo, turned a small-town rivalry into a global celebration of festive brilliance. The Global Glitter Gala lives on today and has expanded globally. The process starts in the month of November and continues through the first week of January. It is a full-time job for Jimmy and Maxwell. The Global Glitter Gala magazine is at a all-time high in subscriptions and advertising dollars. They have added hundreds of staff to execute the global process. In year one alone, there were ten countries participating, which doubled in year two and is steady at around 80 countries today. Woodstock's hotels, restaurants, and shops experience a significant economic boost during the festive season, contributing to the town's growing reputation as the ultimate holiday destination. In addition to creating their annual displays, the Fab Four manage a Maker's Space for folks to learn higher-order Christmas display decorating skills.

The Global Glitter Gala magazine, Italian publication version 2023.

Chapter 7:
Deer Camp Chronicles – Machismo, Mayhem and the Hunt

The Anderson brothers, Mike, Bryan, Kyle, and Jake, eagerly gathered in the cozy hunting shack on the eve of the opening day of the Wisconsin white-tailed deer hunting season. As tradition dictated, they would spend the night together, sharing stories and engaging in their spirited banter. The hunting shack, nestled amidst the winter-clad woods of Rhinelander, stood as a sturdy refuge against the chill. The forest, now adorned with a pristine layer of snow, showcased the silhouettes of the evergreen giants—white pines and red maples—against the wintry canvas. The hunting shack was built by the boys' father, George, and friends, who initially purchased the 120-acre plot of land sometime in the 1950s and constructed the shack with used lumber, propane-fueled appliances and lights, and a potbelly wood stove. George was a formal Yooper, having been born and reared just across the border in Ironwood, MI. An eight-foot-long picnic table with bench seats was centered in the room. Three sets of bunk beds lined the walls. Antlers of past triumphs adorned the walls. A huge hand-drawn map within a makeshift billboard of the 120 acres and surrounding properties hung from another wall in direct view from the picnic table.

The brothers were known for their passionate pursuit of deer, but their approaches to hunting varied greatly. Bryan and Kyle, the middle brothers, were fixated on their high-powered rifles. Convinced that only the most potent and long-reaching firearms could ensure success, they held an unwavering faith in the Barrett .50 caliber sniper rifle. This belief was fueled by Bryan's conviction that the biggest bucks in the area were incredibly intelligent and elusive, necessitating long-range shots of around 250 yards or more from their elevated tree stands. On the other hand, Mike and Jake, the bookends, took a more practical and rational approach. Mike preferred the Remington Model 700, chambered in .270 Winchester, while Jake opted for the classic Winchester Model 94 lever-action rifle in .30-30 Winchester caliber. They believed in the importance of accuracy and maneuverability, selecting rifles that struck a balance between power and practicality.

Throughout the evening, the hunting shack echoed with machismo-laden, satirical, and comedic dialogue between the brothers. Mike and Jake playfully teased Bryan and Kyle, labeling the Barrett rifle an "Elephant Gun" and suggesting its recoil would send them flying out of their tree stands. In retaliation, Ryan and Kyle taunted Mike and Jake about their smaller caliber weapons, questioning their manliness in wielding the mighty Barrett.

Dialogue at the Table (In Yooper Accent):

Mike (scratching his head): "Hey, Bryan, where's that son-in-law o' yours? Ain't he joinin' us this year?"

Bryan (grimacing): "Nah, he's stuck down in Illinois. Damn, FIB couldn't make it this time."

Kyle (raising an eyebrow): "Only thing worse than a freakin' Illinois bastard is a FISHTAB. Musta seen a hundred of those shitheads a towin' der boats back down when I came back from my Chicago trip dis pas fall."

Jake (laughing and nodding): "Freakin' FISHTABs think they own da lakes up here, ya know?"

Bryan (grinning): "Ya know he's a good shit, though. Know what he said – told me when I say let's drink two-tree beers, it is really multiplication caus' we end up drinkin' like a six-pack."

Jake (leaning back, reminiscing): "You guys remember that time when Justin came up here from Illinois? Yeah, he was all gung-ho about bagging a Wisconsin buck. Now, Justin, being a FIB and all, wasn't exactly seasoned in our Northwoods ways."

Bryan (nodding): "Yeah, Justin thought he could out-hunt us Northwoods boys with his fancy gear and all. Little did he know."

Mike (smirking): "So, what happened?"

Kyle (grinning): "Well, imagine this, it's freezing cold, snow up to our knees. There goes Justin, rushing out of the shack in his boxer shorts and boots. Dick a swingin outta that boxer flap. But here's the kicker: he puts on those Lacrosse Cold Snap boots he bought from Cabela's and that orange Stormy Kromer hat he thought was the height of 'Yooper chic.'

The brothers burst into laughter at the image of Justin in his mismatched hunting attire.

Bryan (joining in): "And then, he grabs his rifle off the rack outside der, shoots like five times, misses every shot.

Mike (laughing): "Classic FIB move."

Kyle (smirking): "Wouldn't believe it if I didn't see it. After all that craziness, Justin drops down half-naked dicky-do in the snow and, makes this miraculous two-hundred-yard shot and drops the buck right there. We were all dumbfounded. Swear he left a pecker track and some piss right out der in that snow bank."

Bryan (smiling and wide-eyed): "Yeah, ya know, I wasn't even sure why he was running out the door at first until I saw the rest of the herd of deer scatter from all those shots he ripped off. And I saw those "Tracks in the Snow" by Peter Dragon – could a been a book title."

As the brothers laughed, imagining the absurdity of the scene, the flashback seamlessly integrated into the present, becoming another cherished story in the lore of the Anderson brothers.

Willow Lake, a mile north of the hunting shack now partially frozen at its edges, glistened under the winter sun. A snow-covered trail led from the south end, where the frozen Willow Creek wound its way through the Anderson-owned landscape, connecting the icy shores of the lake to the mighty Wisconsin River downstream. Tamaracks along the creek stood resilient, their golden needles a stark contrast against the snowy surroundings. As dawn broke on opening day, the swamp near the hunting shack transformed into a winter wonderland. Towering eastern hemlocks and balsam firs, their branches dusted with snow, bordered the frozen swamp. Mike and Jake, navigating through the snow-draped forest, passed beneath the skeletal branches of sugar maples, their leaves long gone, leaving behind intricate patterns in the snow. As Jake, retracing his steps from prior successful hunts, walked to his deer stand, the tranquility of the snow-laden woods was shattered as two grouse burst from the foliage, sending him into a startled dance.

Bryan & Kyle with Barrett Rifle

After a nearly half-mile field march, Bryan and Kyle settled into their lofty tree stand, poised to shoot across the swamp at distances that would test the capabilities of their preferred firearm. Mike and Jake, choosing more wooded areas, anticipated bucks sneaking through the trees.

Shortly after sunrise, excitement enveloped the swamp when Bryan spotted a colossal buck, its impressive rack displaying around 8 points. But as he hastily raised the heavy Barrett rifle, his eyes too close to the scope, he fumbled with the weapon and missed the shot. The recoil left a bruise on his right eye and a sore shoulder, prompting him to pass the gun to Kyle.

"Damn, that flipping hurt," Bryan shouted under his breath in silent mode speech.

Mike and Jake, positioned in different sections of the woods, heard the thunderous blast from Bryan's missed shot. Astonished by the deafening sound, they couldn't help but chuckle. Around 40 minutes later, Jake, using his Winchester Model 94, efficiently dispatched a six-point buck from a comfortable distance of 75 yards. Mike, not mistaking the sound of Jake's rifle, felt a tinge of envy.

In the meantime, Mike, perched in his dense section along Willow Creek, noticed an eight-point buck only 50 yards away. With a quick shot, he wounded the deer, but it continued to move. He expertly chambered a new round with the lever action and ultimately brought down the wounded buck. The sound of the Winchester echoed through the woods, reaching the ears of the other brothers. Assuming it was Mike's triumph, they laughed, remarking that the forest sounded like a war zone.

Time pressed on, and both Mike and Jake successfully field-dressed their deer, hanging them proudly from the seemingly ancient pine tree near the hunting shack. They eagerly awaited Bryan and

Kyle's return, listening attentively to the distant rifle shots that reverberated through the landscape.

Meanwhile, Bryan and Jake focused their attention across the swamp. Suddenly, Kyle spotted movement—a massive buck, possibly the largest they had ever seen, emerged from the woods. He counted at least eight points on one side of its majestic rack. Excitement coursed through his veins as he aimed the Barrett rifle, its weight causing his arms to tremble. Bryan reminded him to steady himself on the shooting bar. Aligning the crosshairs on the deer's heart, Kyle squeezed the trigger.

The recoil from the powerful rifle was unforgiving, knocking Kyle off balance and sending him teetering on the edge of the tree stand. Acting swiftly, Bryan grabbed his younger brother by the drawstring of his blaze orange hunting coat, preventing a potentially disastrous fall. Unfortunately, the Barrett slipped from Jake's grasp, tumbling 15 feet to the forest floor. The impact shattered the expensive scope, leaving the rifle damaged beyond repair. As the smoke cleared and they realized they were both safe, a mix of relief and disappointment washed over them.

"Holy fuck! I think I pissed myself!" exclaimed Kyle.

Without delay, Bryan and Kyle descended from the tree stand, retrieving the broken remnants of the Barrett. They hurriedly crossed the swamp, searching for any signs that the shot had connected with the colossal buck. Their hearts sank as they found no blood trail or deer tracks. However, they did notice a freshly broken tree trunk, nearly two inches in diameter, directly in the path where the deer had stood. It became evident that the shot had missed the buck, severing the sugar maple instead. Bryan, concerned, noticed a trickle of blood on Alex's right cheek, evidence of Barrett's powerful recoil scratching his face.

As Bryan and Jake make their way back to the hunting shack, they are met with teasing and laughter from Mike and Jake. The brothers gather around the picnic table, gazing out the sliding glass door, admiring the two deer hanging outside, and the comedic banter ensues.

Bryan (smiling): "Ya know, even if we don't always agree on the rifles, we sure as heck agree on our beer choice."

Mike (chuckling): "And, Johnson's Brats brings us together, even if our rifles threaten to tear us apart."

Jake (raising his bottle): "To the Anderson brothers, the best damn deer hunters and Johnson's Brats eaters in the Northwoods!"

They all take hearty swigs from the brown New Glarus manufactured bottles, the smooth taste of Johnson's Brats adding an extra layer of enjoyment to the evening.

The scent of cooking Johnson's Brats wafted through the hunting shack, mingling with the aroma of Aunt Carol's German potato recipe. The brothers gathered around the potbelly wood stove and shared jokes and memories as they cooked and savored the hearty meal.

Bryan (grinning): "Now, these brats are somethin' else. Johnson's sure knows how to make 'em right!"

Mike (between bites): "Remember that time we camped at High Falls, eh? When we thought we heard The Hodag rustlin' in the woods?"

Jake (laughing): "Turned out it was just Bryan, sleepwalkin' and talkin' some gibberish about a 'Da Turdy Point Buck. That crazy Yoopers song got stuck in his head, ya know.'"

The tales flowed like the Wisconsin River, each story adding to the tapestry of shared experiences. They raised their bottles of Spotted Cow, the clinking sound echoing the bond they held.

Jake (nodding): "And Aunt Carol's potatoes, don't get me started. Pure magic in a pot!"

As they dug into the delicious feast, the shack echoed with laughter and satisfied murmurs. Even the wind outside seemed to join in the celebration, rustling the snow-laden branches of the nearby trees. The boys broke out a Pinochle deck from a drawer in the legacy standing sink and continued the tradition.

Johnson Brats with Aunt Carol's Potato's

Narrator (now in a semi-thick Yooper accent from his exposure to this story telling): Da brothers der ya know, their accents as thick as the snow outside, cherished their hunti' traditions. Not just for the thrill of the chase ya know but for the bonds forged over "two-tree" beers and shared tales of mighty bucks and missed shots. In the heart of Wisconsin's Northwoods, where Da Turdy Point Bucks and the Spotted Cow's graze, the Anderson brothers embodied the spirit of Northwoods camaraderie, where laughter, brotherhood, and a shared love for the outdoors triumphed over machismo and excessive firepower.

The Anderson brothers continue their annual huntin' tradition but with a newfound appreciation for practicality and skill. Bryan sells his broken Barrett rifle and invests in a more suitable firearm, while Jake embraces the importance of stability and positionin' while takin' a shot. In the followin' years, ya know, the brothers share many successful hunts, cherishin' the memories made in the snow-draped woods of Northern Wisconsin. They become known for their satirical and comedic banter, teasin' each other about their rifle choices but ultimately valu'in' the camaraderie and joy of the hunt. And so, the Anderson brothers embody the spirit of the Wisconsin huntin' culture, where laughter, brotherhood, and a shared love for the outdoors triumph over machismo and excessive firepower.

The shack's potbelly stove continued to crackle, casting a warm glow over the table as the brothers raised their bottles once again, toasting another year of successful hunts and enduring brotherhood.

And there, amidst the snow-covered pines and the laughter that echoed through the Northwoods, the legend of the Anderson brothers lived on.

Chapter 8:
Tenderloins, Troubles, and Electric Connections: The Diner Chronicles

In the heart of Kokomo, Indiana, nestled on a corner street, stood Jay's Drive-In, a beloved local diner where blue-collar workers gathered for their weekly lunch meetings. Kokomo is known as the "City of Firsts" for its long history of automotive innovations. Among the list of "firsts" were the first pneumatic rubber tire, the first automotive carburetor, the first mechanical corn picker, and the first commercially built automobile via Haynes-Apperson in 1898. Jay's is known for its tenderloins, proudly claiming in advertisements "Home of Indiana's Largest Tenderloin."

Kokomo Art Association Exhibit 2019 – Impressionist artist RA Whaley

Duke Davis, Frankie Fierce, Rocky Carpenter, and Vinnie Valiant, all long-time friends, frequented the diner, sharing stories and engaging in serious conversations about their recent mishaps.

Kokomo Gazette 1947: Impressionist Image by artist RA Whaley

One sunny afternoon, as the aroma of sizzling burgers filled the air, Duke entered the diner, a determined look on his face, ready to discuss his recent light installation fiasco. Duke, a Journeyman electrician working toward his Master's level certification, took pride in his work. Somewhat a perfectionist, he often expanded work scopes beyond the intention, often resulting in more work and increased work duration. He was batting about .500 on this, having some big wins, some mediocre outcomes, and a few disasters. Duke tended to wear every emotion on his sleeves, so to speak. His self-esteem ebbing and flowing from big wins to other misfortunes.

Duke: "Gentlemen, I must confess the recent light installation in the parking lot has been a nightmare. The lights are flickering, and the brightness is inconsistent. I assure you, it's not my fault. The electrical distribution system is outdated and unable to handle the new bulbs properly."

Frankie, his brows furrowed, leaned forward, ready to express his own frustrations from his experiences as a senior millwright. Frankie had dreams of one day starting his own business as an automation system installer and thus experienced a lot of frustration within his current occupation.

Frankie: "You know, Duke, I can relate. I had a similar experience when I misaligned the conveyor belt system. Parts were tumbling off, production was halted, and it was chaos. But it wasn't my fault. Thosee specs the engineering department gave me were incorrect, leaving me with no choice but to proceed with flawed instructions."

Rocky, a serious expression on his face, nodded in agreement, sharing his own tale of woe.

Rocky: "I understand your struggle, Duke and Frankie. Recently, I poured concrete for a foundation, but the structure ended up uneven and unstable. It was a disaster, but trust me, it wasn't my fault. The architectural plans were flawed, and the engineers failed to provide clear instructions. I was left to interpret vague guidance, and the outcome was beyond my control. You know I do not need this kind of stress. I tend to bring it home. It affects my family life and my enjoyment with the wife and kids."

The atmosphere in Jay's grew more serious as the friends delved into their experiences, each passionately defending their actions and blaming external factors for their respective mishaps. Vinnie, the skilled cook, joined the conversation, his voice filled with empathy.

Vinnie: "I hear you, guys. Mistakes happen, and we must protect our pride. I've had my fair share of mix-ups in the kitchen, serving customers the wrong dishes. But believe me, it's not my fault either. The chaotic environment, lack of proper communication, and even the busy wait staff—everyone plays a part in the confusion. I have way too many irons in the fire. Like I am constantly juggling work and the farm."

The friends nodded in understanding; their bond strengthened by their unwavering belief that they were not at fault. In their eyes, external factors and circumstances beyond their control were to blame for their errors.

As they continued their lunch, the serious yet empathetic conversation echoed through the small cafe, with customers listening in, appreciating the unique perspective and shared experiences of these hardworking individuals. Amid their serious discussion, the camaraderie remained intact, with each friend finding solace in the support of their companions.

*Impressionist Image of Jay's Opening Day –
Kokomo Tribune 1947 – Artist RA Whaley*

Jay's café was built in 1947. An old 1950's-style drive-in with an inside dining room that was added sometime in the 1980s. The dining room is a mixture of tables and booths. One could say it is a bit off the beaten path. Located in a mixed industrial and commercial area of Kokomo, it is one of those places that you likely won't stumble upon unless you are lost. The dining room is on the small side but comfortable, with many pictures of the history of Jay's on the wall. The menu is a mix of traditional food like sandwiches and fries as well as comfort food. On the menu, there are three handmade in-house tenderloins listed which include The King, a Regular tenderloin, and a Mini version. The tenderloins are hand-pounded and breaded, giving them uneven shapes, with the meat being thicker in some places than others. Although off the beaten path, Jay's was a local tenderloin favorite, having tasty and moist meat and exceptional texture. Other favorites are the chicken and noodles lunch platter, which is accompanied by mashed potatoes and gravy, an additional side and a choice of bread. The BLT was another favorite of locals.

Simultaneously, in a booth nearby, Bob, Frankie's supervisor, and Jim, Rocky's supervisor, sat together, glancing over at the group with a mix of annoyance and amusement. They proceeded to eat their mini tenderloins and wash the moist meat down with Double Cola's.

Bob: leaning in closer, his voice low, "Jim, would you take a look at those guys over there? Duke, Frankie, Rocky, and Vinnie. I tell you, they are a bunch of dumbasses. Always finding excuses, never taking responsibility for their mistakes."

Jim, chuckling softly, nodded in agreement, observing the antics of the group.

Jim: "You're right, Bob. Duke thinks he's some kind of electrical genius, but all he's doing is creating more problems. Remember when he was tasked with replacing the parking lot lights with new bulbs? He thought he could rewire the entire electrical distribution panel without proper planning. The result? Flickering lights all over the place."

Bob: "Oh, I know, Jim. It was a disaster. He didn't realize that the existing system couldn't handle the load of the new bulbs. Instead of accepting his error, he blamed the lights themselves, claiming they were inferior. Typical Duke."

Jim: "And Frankie, don't even get me started. He's been misaligning things ever since he started working here. Remember when he was assigned to maintain the conveyor belt system? One small misalignment led to a catastrophic production line disaster. It cost the company time money, and damaged our reputation."

Bob: "Absolutely, Jim. It was a nightmare. He blamed his colleagues, saying they didn't provide accurate measurements or blueprints. But it was his lack of attention to detail that caused the chaos. It's always someone else's fault in Frankie's world. Like, we need this kind of shit happening; it is hard enough to keep the factory pumped with work. Disasters like this make corporate question our viability. Times are tough; we all need to keep our jobs."

Jim: "And Rocky, oh boy. He managed to pour an uneven and unstable foundation for that building section. It was a disaster waiting to happen. The architectural plans were crystal clear, but he insists the fault lies with the engineers. He claimed they provided vague instructions, leaving him to interpret their intentions. What a load of nonsense. I will admit, though, with all these corporate cost-cutting measures going on, I wonder if folks in Detroit are dropping the ball."

Bob: "Couldn't agree more, Jim. Rocky's lack of accountability is infuriating. We had to spend extra time and money fixing his mess, all because he couldn't admit his own shortcomings. And don't even get me started on Vinnie's mix-ups in the kitchen."

Jim: "Ah, Vinnie. He once spilled hot soup on a customer, resulting in severe burns and a lawsuit against the restaurant. Instead of accepting his mistake, he blamed the lack of training and proper equipment. But let's face it, his absent-mindedness and lack of attention to detail were the real culprits behind the incident."

As Bob and Jim continued their private conversation, their frustration with Duke, Frankie, Rocky, and Vinnie's refusal to acknowledge their faults remained evident. The background stories shed light on the circumstances surrounding their major fuckups, emphasizing their lack of accountability and the impact it had on their respective jobs.

Clara: "Excuse me, gentlemen," she said, her voice carrying a blend of kindness and authority, "I've been listening to your conversation, and I couldn't help but notice you seem pretty frustrated with those guys over there."

Bob and Jim looked at each other, somewhat surprised, but nodded in agreement.

Clara: "You know, I've been working here longer than I can remember, and I've seen all kinds of folks come and go. I've learned that everyone has their strengths and weaknesses, but what really matters is how we handle them. It's easy to blame others when things go wrong, but it takes real character to look at the bigger picture."

She paused, allowing her words to sink in before continuing. "Duke, Frankie, Rocky, and Vinnie, they're good men at heart. They might make mistakes, but they're out there trying their best. Sometimes, they just need a little guidance and support to get back on track. And that's where you come in. Instead of just criticizing them, maybe try to understand their struggles and help them grow. A little patience and mentorship can go a long way."

Clara smiled warmly, her eyes filled with the wisdom of years. "Remember, we're all in this together. Times are tough for everyone, and we all need a little help now and then. Give them a chance to learn from their mistakes and to prove their worth. You might be surprised at what they can achieve with the right support."

Bob and Jim sat in thoughtful silence, absorbing Clara's advice. They exchanged glances, realizing that perhaps they had been too quick to judge and too harsh in their assessments.

Clara: "Now, how about I get you boys some two more Mini's On the house, this time. A little food for thought and a full belly never hurt anyone."

As Clara walked away to fetch their order, Bob and Jim found themselves reflecting on her words, considering how they might change their approach to help their team succeed.

Across the diner, the oblivious quartet carried on with their animated discussion, unaware of the supervisors' judgment and private criticisms. The divergent perspectives of the workers and their supervisors showcased the stark contrast in accountability and the differing perceptions of their actions.

Jay's Drive In – Kokomo, IN 2024

In Jay's Drive-In, amidst the clatter of plates and the laughter of patrons, two conversations had unfolded simultaneously—one filled with camaraderie, blame-shifting, and self-assuredness, and the other brimming with frustration and a longing for greater accountability.

Jay's son, Raymond, was like an oracle to these struggles. Raymond continued to manage the daily operations and listened intently to his customers. Like a character in a Steinbeck novel, he could see his customer's internal conflicts that drive their actions. The inner turmoil that each grappled with in their successes and failures and the external blame they placed.

Raymond leaned against the counter, a thoughtful expression on his face. He had seen many men like Duke, Frankie, Rocky, and Vinnie pass through Jay's Drive-In over the years, each with their own struggles and triumphs. As he listened to their conversation, he decided it was time to share a piece of wisdom passed down from his father.

"You know, fellas," Raymond began, his voice steady and warm, "My father used to say that life's like working on an old car. Sometimes, it runs smooth, sometimes it breaks down, and a lot of times, it's a struggle to keep it going. But the key isn't just in blaming the parts that don't fit or the tools that don't work. The key is in the effort you put in to understand the problem and fix it together."

He paused, letting the words sink in, before continuing. "We all have our share of mishaps, and it's easy to point fingers at things we can't control. But if you want to keep that old car running, you've got to take a good, hard look at what you can do better. Sometimes, it means swallowing your pride and asking for help. Other times, it's about taking responsibility and learning from those mistakes. But most importantly, it's about sticking together because no one gets through the tough times alone."

Raymond smiled gently at the group. "So, next time things go wrong, remember that you've got each other and that every challenge is a chance to grow. My father believed that, and it's what kept this place going all these years. And maybe, just maybe, it's what will keep you all moving forward, too."

As the group prepared to leave and head back to work, the familiar camaraderie wrapped around them like an old, comfortable coat. They walked out of Jay's, ready to tackle the rest of the day, but fate had other plans. Just a block away from the diner, a loud crash echoed through the streets.

A semi-truck had collided with a power pole, sending it crashing down onto a car below. The live electric wires draped over the vehicle, crackling ominously. Inside the car, a man clutched his chest, his face contorted in pain, while his wife screamed for help.

The Kokomo Tribune: Circa 2020

Duke, with his electrician's instincts kicking in, shouted a warning as Bob and Jim instinctively moved toward the car. "Stop! Those wires are live! You'll get electrocuted if you touch the car!"

Bob and Jim froze, realizing the gravity of the situation. Rocky, quick on his feet, ran to his truck and grabbed some two-by-fours.

Using the wooden boards as insulators, he carefully pushed the wires off the car.

Frankie, agile and decisive, moved in as soon as the wires were clear, pulling the man out of the car with practiced efficiency. The man's condition was dire; his breath was shallow and erratic. Frankie, who had been observing with mounting concern, remembered the CPR training he had recently undergone at work as part of his safety committee role. Under Frankie's direction, Frankie and Vinnie immediately began performing CPR on the man, their actions synchronized and urgent.

As the minutes ticked by, their efforts seemed to pay off. The man's breathing steadied, and he began to show signs of regaining consciousness. His wife, tears streaming down her face, watched with a mixture of hope and fear.

Bob and Jim, witnessing the teamwork and bravery of their subordinates, felt a shift in their perception. Clara's words echoed in their minds, reminding them of the potential for growth and redemption in everyone.

As the ambulance arrived and took over, the group stood back, panting and adrenaline-fueled. The man's wife turned to them, gratitude and relief written all over her face. "Thank you. You saved his life. Thank you so much."

Duke, Frankie, Rocky, and Vinnie exchanged glances, a newfound respect and understanding passing between them. For a moment, their usual banter and bravado were replaced by a solemn recognition of their capabilities and the importance of their work.

Bob approached the group, his demeanor softer, his voice tinged with respect. "You guys did good today. Real good. Maybe we've been too hard on you. Let's get back to work, but know this—we see what you're capable of. Let's build on that."

Jim nodded in agreement; his earlier frustration was replaced with a sense of pride in his team. "Yeah, what Bob said. You all showed what you're made of today. Let's carry that forward."

As they headed back to the factory, the group walked with a new sense of purpose. The events of the day had forged a stronger bond between them, bridging the gap between the workers and their supervisors. In the heart of Kokomo, amidst the echoes of automotive history and the familiar hum of Jay's Drive-In, a moment of crisis had brought out the best in everyone, revealing the true strength of their community.

Chapter 9:
When Machismo Meets Wokeness at the Woodward Dream Cruise

As the sun beat down on the scorching pavement of Woodward Avenue, Bruce and Roy sat side by side, their pride and joy muscle cars parked nearby. It had been four long years since they last saw each other, and their excitement was palpable. The unmistakable aroma of burning rubber and high-octane fuel hung in the air, matching the exhilaration building between the two friends.

Bruce, his towering figure exuding machismo, leaned back against the plush leather seats of his 1967 Chevelle SS. His broad shoulders stretched the fabric of his favorite muscle car t-shirt as he eagerly recounted the upgrades he had made to his beloved Chevy.

Bruce and his Legendary 67 Chevelle

"Roy, my friend, you won't believe the muscle I've injected into my Chevelle," Bruce declared, a twinkle of pride in his eyes. "I've swapped that standard 396 cu inch V8 for that monster ZZ502 crate engine. It roars like a beast now!"

Roy, a fellow devotee of all things macho, leaned forward in his 2010 Dodge Challenger. His grin widened as he heard Bruce's words, eager to share his own automotive triumphs. "Well, Bruce, you know I had to step up my game too," Roy replied with a smirk. "I've added a cold air intake and performance headers to my Challenger, pushing the horsepower to a respectable 387. But I'm not stopping there. I want that 425 horsepower of the 6.1-liter Hemi engine."

Bruce nodded approvingly, his bearded chin jutting forward. "Ah, Roy, always striving for more power! That's the spirit, my man!" He playfully punched Roy's arm, the impact echoing like thunder.

Their car club friends, gathered around them, joined in the banter, each showcasing their own automotive conquests. Bruce's fellow Early Times Street Rods members boasted about their impressive rides, sharing tales of horsepower upgrades, wheel and tire combinations, and eye-catching paint jobs.

Woodward Avenue downtown Detroit, MI circa 2010

As the conversation continued, the air filled with laughter and good-natured ribbing. The men traded stories of burnouts, drag races, and the sheer thrill of owning these magnificent machines. Their camaraderie was fueled by their shared passion for muscle cars and their unyielding machismo.

"But hey, Bruce," Roy interjected with a sly grin, "Have you seen my Cragar wheels and RT racing stripes? They give my Challenger that vintage '70s muscle car look. You can't deny the sheer macho charm!"

Bruce let out a hearty laugh, slapping Roy on the back. "You're right, my friend! Your Challenger does look like a beast from the past. It's almost as impressive as my Chevelle's shiny chrome grille and wide tires that grip the road like it owes them. "That's so money!" replied Roy.

Their banter carried on, punctuated by bursts of laughter and exclamations of machismo. The sun dipped lower on the horizon, casting a warm orange glow over the classic metal frames before them. The Woodward Dream Cruise was in full swing, and amidst the roaring engines and cheering crowds, Bruce and Roy reveled in their shared passion and brotherhood.

As the conversation between Bruce and Roy carried on, their banter filling the air, a voice unexpectedly chimed in. Tim, the rational banker from Huntington Bank, approached the group, drawn by the excitement of the Dream Cruise and the spectacle of the magnificent muscle cars.

"Hey there, guys! Mind if I join in?" Tim asked with a friendly smile, looking at the group of machismo-laden car enthusiasts.

Bruce's bushy eyebrows arched in surprise, and he exchanged a knowing glance with Roy. Tim's presence seemed incongruous amidst the backdrop of roaring engines and testosterone-fueled conversations. Nonetheless, Bruce, ever the embodiment of manliness, welcomed Tim with a polite nod.

"Sure thing, Tim. Pull up a seat and soak in the glory of these magnificent machines," Bruce replied, his voice dripping with a mix of amusement and curiosity.

Tim, seemingly unfazed by the snickers and masculinity that surrounded him, took a deep breath and ventured into the conversation. "I must admit, I appreciate the craftsmanship and the artistry of these cars. But I can't help but wonder, isn't the pursuit of more horsepower and muscle a bit... well, absurd?"

A wave of stifled laughter rippled through the group, but Roy, ever the diplomat, stepped in to offer a polite response. "Tim, my friend, we understand your perspective. We all have our own passions and interests. For us, these muscle cars embody power, beauty, and a sense of freedom. It's about more than just horsepower; it's about the sheer joy of driving and the thrill of the open road."

Detroit, MI Jefferson Street prior to 2023 Detroit Grand Prix

Bruce, unable to resist the opportunity to poke fun, chimed in with a grin. "Come on, Tim. Where's your sense of adventure? Can't you feel the rumble of these engines in your chest? It's the call of the wild, my friend."

Tim chuckled, his eyes glinting with a touch of wry humor. "I can appreciate the appeal, Bruce. But as a banker, I find myself drawn to efficiency and practicality. My trusty Honda Accord gets me from point A to point B without any need for excess horsepower or muscly aesthetics."

Bruce, Roy, and a few members of the Early Times Street Rod car crew exchanged amused glances, unable to fully comprehend Tim's pragmatic outlook. But they respected his perspective and admired his willingness to engage in the conversation.

Roy raised his hand as if surrendering to Tim's rationality. "Fair enough, Tim. We all have our own preferences, and that's what makes the world interesting. But just remember, sometimes it's good to let loose, embrace the raw power, and experience life in the fast lane."

Tim nodded appreciatively, acknowledging the diversity of interests within the group. He may not share their thirst for horsepower and muscle, but he valued their passion and dedication to their craft.

As Tim continued in the conversation, he couldn't help but notice the undeniable machismo in the air. He gathered his thoughts, ready to offer a different perspective, one that embraced the attributes of a woke viewpoint. The car club gallery, however, couldn't help but snicker, already sensing the clash of ideologies about to unfold.

Tim cleared his throat and spoke, his voice laced with a gentle determination. "You know, guys, while I admire the power and beauty of these muscle cars, it's essential to consider the broader impact of our choices. We can still enjoy our love for automobiles while being conscious of environmental sustainability and social responsibility."

A few stifled chuckles emanated from the car club gallery, the idea of reconciling machismo and "woke" viewpoints appearing incongruous to their ears. But Tim, undeterred, continued.

"Empathy and critical thinking play vital roles here. We should strive to understand how our choices impact the world around us. The excessive horsepower and fuel consumption of these cars contribute to pollution and climate change. It's important to consider more sustainable options and reduce our carbon footprints for the sake of future generations."

Bruce, Roy, and the others exchanged skeptical glances, their machismo pride tinged with amusement. Bruce couldn't resist a sly grin as he retorted, "Come on, Tim, you're raining on our horsepower parade! We love the thrill, the power, and the freedom these cars represent. It's about embracing life to the fullest!"

More snickers emerged from the gallery, the tension between machismo and "woke" viewpoints palpable. But Tim, drawing strength from his convictions, held his ground.

"Absolutely, Bruce. I understand the appeal, and there's no denying the excitement. But let's also explore ways to strike a balance, to find joy in vehicles that are environmentally friendly or support social causes. We can still appreciate beauty, craftsmanship, and performance while being conscious of the greater impact."

Roy, ever the mediator, interjected with a thoughtful expression. "Tim, I hear you. It's about finding that middle ground, where our passions and values intersect. Perhaps there are ways to modify our cars, consider alternative energy sources, or support initiatives that promote sustainability within our shared love for automotive culture."

The snickers from the car club gallery began to subside as the conversation shifted from mockery to reflection. While differences remained, a newfound respect for Tim's perspective emerged, recognizing the importance of considering the greater implications of their passion.

As the conversation shifted towards finding common ground between machismo and "woke" perspectives, Roy's curiosity was piqued by Tim's mention of sustainability. He turned to Tim with a mischievous grin.

"You know, Tim, electrifying a muscle car could be the perfect blend of our worlds. Imagine the power of an electric motor coupled with the iconic design of a classic muscle car," Roy proposed, a glimmer of excitement in his eyes.

Tim raised an eyebrow, intrigued by the suggestion. "That's an interesting idea, Roy. I never considered electrifying a muscle car before. It could be a game-changer in terms of sustainability and environmental impact. But, honestly, I'm more drawn to old trucks, like the Chevy C10."

A smile spread across Roy's face, his mind racing with possibilities. "Ah, the Chevy C10, a classic beauty. Tim, my friend, have you ever thought about electrifying an old truck? Imagine the retro charm combined with the eco-consciousness of an electric powertrain. It could be a standout at the Dream Cruise!"

Tim's eyes widened with excitement. "That's an incredible suggestion, Roy. I do love old Chevy trucks and electrifying one would be a fantastic way to embrace sustainability and still indulge in the automotive passion we all share. I could join you at the Woodward Dream Cruise with my electrified Chevy C10!"

The car club gallery, initially skeptical, began to see the possibilities in this unexpected collaboration between machismo and "woke" ideologies. The conversations buzzed with newfound enthusiasm, exploring the realm of electric muscle cars and retrofitted trucks.

As the Woodward Dream Cruise drew closer to its culmination, the group's discussions evolved into plans and dreams of a future where classic muscle cars and trucks could embrace sustainable technologies. The once-divergent perspectives now danced in harmony, driven by a shared desire to preserve the automotive heritage while embracing a greener future.

Roy, Bruce, Tim, and the rest of the car club members forged a bond that transcended their initial differences. They realized that by combining their passions, they could contribute to a better world and still revel in the thrill of the Dream Cruise.

And so, their imaginations ignited with possibilities, the machismo and "woke" perspectives intertwined to shape a future where electrified muscle cars and retrofitted trucks stood side by side, the embodiment of power, nostalgia, and sustainability.

As the Woodward Dream Cruise continued to unfold, Bruce and Roy found themselves engrossed in a conversation about their families and the memories they had created together back in Hampshire, Illinois. The roar of the engines served as the backdrop to their heartfelt reminiscing.

"Remember when we used to take the kids to the Suds and Fun Rod Run?" Bruce asked, a nostalgic smile playing on his lips.

Roy nodded, a hint of sentimentality in his eyes. "Oh, those were the days, Bruce. Our families together, enjoying the sights and sounds of classic cars. It was a true bonding experience."

Just as they delved deeper into their memories, a familiar voice interrupted their conversation. "Hey, Dad! Bruce!" It was Jason, Bruce's son, who had just arrived from Illinois, joining their conversation midstream.

Bruce's face lit up with joy as he embraced his son. "Jason, my boy! It's been too long. Glad you could join us here in Michigan."

Jason returned the embrace, a mix of excitement and confusion in his eyes. "Yeah, Dad. The Woodward Dream Cruise is legendary. But who's this guy?" he pointed at Tim, a slight air of machismo lacing his words.

Bruce chuckled, introducing Tim to Jason. "This is Tim, a friend we've made here at the Dream Cruise. He's more of a practical guy, not quite in tune with our love for muscle cars. But hey, different strokes for different folks, right?"

As Tim and Jason exchanged polite nods, their contrasting perspectives apparent, Jason's eyes wandered to the parking lot. His gaze landed on Tim's 2001 Honda Accord, and a smirk tugged at the corners of his mouth. Unable to resist the machismo inherited from his father, he made a playful comment.

"Well, Tim, that piece of shit you're driving doesn't quite fit in here with these magnificent machines, does it?" Jason's words dripped with good-natured jest, reflecting the banter and machismo that ran through his veins.

Roy and Bruce burst into laughter, recognizing Jason's playful teasing. "Easy there, Jason! Let's keep it friendly," Roy interjected, a glint of amusement in his eyes.

Tim, though initially taken aback, took the comment in stride. "Hey, it may not be a muscle car, but it gets the job done," he replied, offering a good-natured shrug.

The group shared a laugh; the camaraderie was strengthened by their ability to appreciate each other's differences. The love for cars, family, and the excitement of the Dream Cruise bridged the gap between their contrasting perspectives.

Woodward Avenue near Pontiac, MI

As the conversation carried on, Bruce, Roy, Jason, and Tim found common ground in their shared passion for the automotive world.

Stories flowed, memories were shared, and in the midst of roaring engines and the smell of burning rubber, a unique bond was forged—a bond that celebrated both the machismo of muscle cars and the practicality of other modes of transportation.

And as the Woodward Dream Cruise drew to a close, the group reflected on the day's events, cherishing the memories created and the laughter shared. The machismo, the wokeness, and the playful banter had coexisted harmoniously, creating a mosaic of perspectives that made their experience richer.

As they bid each other farewell, Bruce, Roy, Jason, and Tim knew that their paths may diverge, but the shared love for cars, family, and the spirit of camaraderie would forever bind them together, leaving a lasting impression as solid as the engines that roared down Woodward Avenue.

Chapter 10:
Smoky Texas Bonds and the Legendary Weber

Written By: Troy Lindner and Rob Whaley

Texas summer days are always hot. On this afternoon, four neighbors settled onto Sheriff's backyard patio to quench their thirst and prepare for a barbecue feast. Dale 'Sheriff' Cunningham had an infectious enthusiasm for life. His loud, booming laugh drew in everyone around him, and his sharp wit often kept friends on their toes. Sheriff inherited his love for barbecue from his father, a local sheriff known for his larger-than-life presence. After his father passed away, Dale took over the family tradition of hosting backyard barbecues, using the same smoker his father did, seasoned with decades of memories.

The four friends comfortably settled on the Sheriff's patio, prepping their meat and telling stories. The conversation flowed easily and stretched on as long as the shadows on the patio. With a flick of his lighter, Sheriff ignited the smoker, and the tantalizing aromas filled the warm summer air. Whispered mumbles of approval came from around the patio as the meats sizzled and sputtered.

Sheriff's patio

"I know you guys love your fancy backyards and outdoor pizza ovens and whatever, but the decades of seasoning on my dad's smoker bring out the flavor in everything I cook!" said Sheriff. "This is a one and only original Weber. A history forged in steel. It started as a grill and evolved it into a smoker. I told y'all Pops was friends with Georgie Stephen, and he made this for Pops. I betcha' this thing here is pushin' 70 years old. Had to make a few modifications over the years, blast her, repaint, but she is still cookin" Continued Sheriff.

Sheriff's Legendary Weber

"You're crazy, Sheriff!" shouted Rick Thompson. Originally from Chicago, which is home to the Weber company, Rick moved to Texas from an IT job at the Chicago Board of Trade for one with a prominent automotive OEM. An excitable type, Rick swore by his high-tech smoker, equipped with Wi-Fi capabilities that allowed him to monitor and control the temperature from his smartphone. "You can't beat a modern smoker when it comes to barbecue! Those tech guys have thought of everything! Briskets practically cook themselves, and they're perfect. Every. Single. Time." he exclaimed. Rick's passion for perfection was his very own pursuit, and it often intensified the discussions that followed. I practically lived down the road from the Weber factory in Huntley.

"Well, I think you're discounting the quality of the meat," Jimbo interjected. Jim "Jimbo" Martinez, the stoic member of the group, had a sharp tongue and countered the claim. His practical nature and keen eye for detail meant that he was always able to add an interesting perspective. Jimbo worked as a butcher at the local grocery store and had a deep appreciation for high-quality meat. His father was a rancher, and he grew up learning the intricacies of cattle raising and meat selection. "There's no way that you're going to get a perfect brisket unless you start with a good cut of meat. Oh, and just to be clear, my new traditional offset smoker will out-cook your tech gadget any day," he delivered with a smile.

Jimbo's meat counter

Of course, a retort had to follow. With an exuberant chuckle, Denny shouted, "If you properly marinate and season mid-grade pork, the result will crush your high-end cuts. I'm just sayin'." Denny Lewis, the joker of the group, was known for his mischievous sense of humor and laid-back attitude. He worked as a high school history teacher, a job he loved because it allowed him to inspire young minds while indulging in his love for storytelling. Denny was also known for his secret marinade recipes, which he guarded closely. His mischievous sense of humor easily found its way into the conversations and helped to keep the fun simmering all night. He continued his comedic rant: "You guys, with all your smoker-style talk. Oh, my offset, oh my bullet is better, no you gotta' use a vertical rig, well I only use drums, oh I use pellets. Blah, blah, blah."

"Umm… not," Jimbo replied. "But whatever. Hey—hand me a beer!"

The conversation circled amongst the friends, each trying to outdo the others for a few more moments until the Sheriff's announcement of "smoker's ready!" Like magic, silence overtook the crew as the first bites went down. Warm comments like "very good" and "great work" flowed easily, and not a question or mention of "the cut," "the smoker," or any other detail. A simple, heartfelt meal made by a good friend outshined any need to discuss it any further. These were outstanding barbecue meats—no matter which smoker was used.

As the evening progressed and the sun dipped below the horizon, casting long shadows across the backyard, Sheriff leaned back in his chair, a thoughtful look on his face. "You know, there's that barbecue contest next month. How about we all enter and see whose method really is the best?" The challenge hung in the warm air, a new layer of friendly competition sparking between them.

Rick, fiddling with his smartphone to adjust the smoker's settings, perked up. "Now that sounds like a plan. I've been wanting to put my high-tech smoker's capabilities to the real test."

Jimbo nodded slowly, a hint of a smile playing at the corners of his mouth. "I'm in. It'll be good to show everyone what a well-cut piece of meat can do."

Denny raised his beer in agreement, his eyes twinkling with mischief. "Count me in too. I've got a few new marinade tricks up my sleeve that will blow your minds."

Denny the master marinator in action

In the weeks leading up to the competition, each friend prepared in his own way. The sheriff continued using his father's old smoker, perfecting his timing and flavors. But he often found himself reminiscing about his father, feeling the weight of his legacy more than ever.

One evening, as Sheriff cleaned the old smoker, Rick stopped by. "Hey, Sheriff, I've been thinking about the competition. You know, my dad wasn't into barbecue, but he was a tech whiz. Maybe that's why I'm so into this stuff." Rick's eyes gleamed as he held up his smartphone. "But maybe I've been too focused on the tech and not enough on what really matters."

Sheriff smiled, clapping Rick on the shoulder. "It's about the balance, Rick. The technology's great, but it's the heart that makes it special."

Rick nodded, understanding dawning in his eyes. "You're right. I think I'll spend more time enjoying the process, not just the results."

Meanwhile, Jimbo was spending more time at the butcher shop, selecting the finest cuts of meat and practicing his slow-cooking skills with a precision that came from years of experience. He also mulled over the future of his family's ranch, considering the possibility of entering the competition as a way to boost its reputation. One afternoon, he mentioned his concerns to Denny, who was mixing a new marinade.

"I've been thinking about the ranch," Jimbo said quietly. "It's been in my family for generations, but things have been tough lately."

Jimbo's ranch

Denny, sensing the seriousness of the conversation, put down his mixing bowl. "Jimbo, you've got a gift. Your knowledge, your skill with meat – that's something special. Maybe this competition is exactly what you need to remind folks what the ranch stands for."

Jimbo smiled, a rare sight. "Thanks, Denny. I needed to hear that."

Denny, on the other hand, was both excited and nervous. Beyond the competition, he was preparing to propose to his longtime girlfriend, Jenny. His friends noticed his distraction during their gatherings and began offering advice, both sincere and humorous, helping him find the confidence he needed.

One night, as the friends were sitting around the smoker, Denny blurted out, "Guys, I'm going to ask Jenny to marry me." The group fell silent for a moment, then erupted in cheers and claps.

"About time!" Sheriff laughed. "You'll do great, Denny. Just be yourself."

"Yeah, and don't overthink it," Rick added, grinning. "You've got this."

Jimbo nodded, adding, "She's a lucky lady, Denny."

With the encouragement of his friends, Denny felt a renewed sense of confidence.

The day of the barbecue competition arrived, and the town was buzzing with excitement. Booths were set up, smokers fired, and the tantalizing scent of barbecue filled the air. The friends arrived together, each setting up their station with a mix of camaraderie and competitive spirit.

Sheriff's setup was simple but steeped in tradition. His father's old smoker stood proudly, its surface seasoned with years of memories. Rick's station was a tech marvel, complete with his Wi-Fi-enabled smoker and a laptop to monitor the cooking process. Jimbo's area was meticulously organized, showcasing an array of premium cuts of meat. Denny's booth, decorated with an eclectic mix of spices and sauces, drew curious onlookers with its bold, enticing aromas.

As the competition began, the friends fell into a rhythm, each showcasing their unique approach. Sheriff's steady, confident manner drew a crowd, his stories and laughter as much a part of the show as his barbecue. Rick's precise, tech-driven method fascinated onlookers, who marveled at his ability to control the smoker from his phone. Jimbo's expertise in meat selection and slow-cooking technique impressed judges and spectators alike, while Denny's vibrant personality and innovative marinades added a playful twist to the event.

Throughout the day, the friends found moments to visit each other's booths, sharing tips, tasting samples, and offering encouragement. Their camaraderie was evident, their competitive banter light-hearted and filled with mutual respect.

As the judges made their rounds, tasting and evaluating, the friends couldn't help but glance at each other's booths, offering silent nods of encouragement. When the results were finally announced, the friends stood together, awaiting the verdict.

"In third place, for his innovative use of technology in barbecue, Rick Thompson!" Rick's face lit up as he accepted his ribbon, giving his friends a triumphant grin.

"In second place, for his exceptional cuts of meat and grilling technique, Jim Martinez!" Jimbo smiled broadly, tipping his hat to the crowd as he shook hands with the judges.

"And in the first place, for his outstanding flavors and sense of tradition, Dale 'Sheriff' Cunningham!" Sheriff's booming laugh echoed through the crowd as he accepted his trophy, lifting it high in the air.

That evening, the friends gathered with their significant others once more in Sheriff's backyard, the competition behind them. They sat around the old smoker, sharing stories and laughter, their bonds stronger than ever. Sheriff looked around at his friends, a sense of pride and contentment washing over him.

"You know," Sheriff said, raising his beer, "it's not just about the smoker, or the meat, or even the tech. It's about the people you share it with. My old man taught me that, and today just proved it."

Rick nodded a newfound appreciation in his eyes. "I've always thought perfection was in the details, but now I see it's also in the company."

Jimbo, reflecting on the day's events and his decision to keep the family ranch, added, "And in the traditions we carry forward, blending the old with the new."

Denny, smiling with a secret satisfaction, knew he had found the right moment. "Speaking of company," he began, "I have an announcement. Jenny, would you come here for a second?"

Jenny joined them, curiosity in her eyes. Denny took a deep breath, then dropped to one knee, pulling out a ring. "Jenny, will you marry me?"

Tears welled up in Jenny's eyes as she nodded, "Yes, Denny, of course!"

Denny and Jenny

Cheers erupted around the patio as the friends celebrated Denny's proposal, their laughter and joy filling the warm summer night.

And so, under the Texas stars, they continued their tradition, not just of barbecue but of friendship, love, and the shared moments that make life truly flavorful.

Epilogue:

Months later, the friends reflected on how the competition had changed them. The sheriff continued to host their gatherings, each one a testament to his father's legacy and the bonds they shared. Rick found a balance between technology and the human touch, enriching his barbecue experience and his friendships. Jimbo saw the ranch thrive with renewed interest and support, and he felt a deeper connection to his heritage. Denny, now happily engaged, felt more confident and grateful for the love and camaraderie in his life.

The competition had been more than just about barbecue; it had been a journey of growth, connection, and understanding. And in the heart of Texas, their friendship burned brighter than ever.

Bonus Chapter: Arlington Chronicles – Tales from the Links with Big Ray and Keith

Written by: Donn Johnson and Rob Whaley

Ah, the summer of '79—a time when the air was thick with the promise of adventure and the scent of freshly cut grass. It was during this halcyon season that my dear friend Keith Cox and I, fueled by an insatiable passion for the game of golf, found ourselves drawn into the orbit of none other than Big Ray, the venerable golf professional of Arlington Country Club.

Now, allow me to paint you a picture of Big Ray—a man as formidable as he was charismatic, with a personality as colorful as the Kentucky sky at dusk. With a cigarette or cigar forever clutched between his weathered fingers, Big Ray cut a striking figure against the backdrop of the fairways, his Southern drawl and penchant for the word "son" lending an air of authority to his every utterance.

Big Ray at Arlington CC

But make no mistake—behind that easygoing demeanor lay a wealth of knowledge and experience honed over the years spent on the links. Big Ray was more than just a golf pro; he was a mentor, a sage, and a font of wisdom for those willing to listen. And listen, we did, hanging on his every word as he dispensed pearls of golfing wisdom with the ease of a seasoned raconteur.

Indeed, it was under Big Ray's tutelage that Keith and I honed our skills on the course, guided by his sage advice and unwavering encouragement. Whether admonishing us to "keep our heads back" or "keep our heads down," Big Ray had a knack for getting his point across in a way that left an indelible impression.

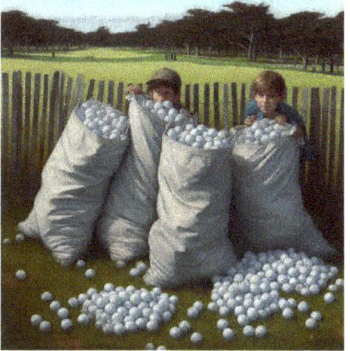

And so it was that with Big Ray's guidance, we embarked on a journey of discovery—a journey that would take us to the very depths of Arlington's lakes in search of lost golf balls and hidden treasures. Little did we know that our misadventures would lead us down a path fraught with mischief, mayhem, and more than a few laughs along the way.

But that, dear reader, is a tale for another time—a tale of friendship, folly, and the enduring allure of the game of golf. For now, let us raise our glasses to Big Ray, the Southern gentleman whose wisdom and wit left an indelible mark on our lives, and to the countless adventures that await us on the fairways and greens of Arlington Country Club.

1979 left its mark on Kentucky like a well-worn divot on the green. With inflation soaring, gas prices skyrocketing, and interest rates climbing to dizzying heights, it was a time when even the humble golf ball found itself priced beyond reach. And yet, despite the economic turmoil that gripped the nation, my dear friend Keith Cox and I remained undeterred in our pursuit of the perfect swing.

Our journey began in the summer of '77, two young lads with a shared love for the game and a penchant for mischief. From the moment our cleats touched the hallowed grounds of Arlington Country Club, we were hooked—hooked on the thrill of the game, the camaraderie of the clubhouse, and the promise of adventure that lurked around every dogleg.

But oh, how those lakes tormented us! Like sirens of the fairways, they beckoned with deceptive allure, luring unsuspecting golf balls to their watery depths with each errant shot. And Keith and I, eager young players with dreams of greatness, fell victim time and time again to their treacherous charms.

It was a ritual as timeless as the game itself: rise with the dawn, make the pilgrimage to Arlington, and embark on a marathon of golf that would put even the hardiest of players to shame. From the first light of morning until the sweltering heat of midday forced us to seek refuge in the cool waters of the pool, we played with the unbridled enthusiasm of youth, heedless of the toll it would take on our dwindling supply of golf balls.

Those were the days—days filled with sun-soaked fairways, laughter that echoed across the greens, and the occasional expletive muttered under one's breath as yet another ball found its watery grave. But through it all, Keith and I persevered, our spirits undaunted by the challenges that lay before us and our determination unwavering in the face of adversity.

And so, as we reflect on that fateful summer of '79, let us raise our clubs in salute to the indomitable spirit of youth, to the enduring bond of friendship, and to the game of golf—a game that, despite its many trials and tribulations, continues to captivate and inspire us to this day.

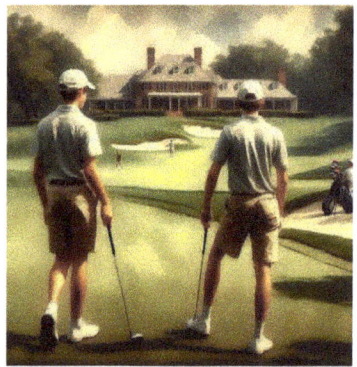

Donn and Keith Arlington CC 1979

Picture it: a sultry summer morning at Arlington Country Club, the air thick with the promise of another day on the links. There we stood, Keith Cox and I, gazing out over the shimmering expanse of the fourth hole, its placid surface belying the treacherous depths that lay beneath. It was a mere 150 yards to clear the lake—or so the scorecard claimed—but to our beleaguered minds, it might as well have been a mile.

With each errant swing, another golf ball met its watery demise, disappearing into the depths with a mournful splash that echoed our frustration. Oh, how we cursed that accursed lake, it's siren song luring us to our doom time and time again.

But on this morning, as we stood on the precipice of yet another lost ball, Keith uttered a question that would change the course of our fate: "How many golf balls do you think are in that lake, Donn?" The query hung in the air like a tantalizing challenge, stirring something deep within me.

As I pondered the sheer magnitude of our collective losses—200 balls? 300? —Keith's proposal struck me with the force of a revelation. "What if we can cut a deal with Big Ray to go in there and get the golf balls?" he suggested, his eyes alight with the spark of possibility.

And in that moment, I knew that redemption was within our grasp. With a nod and a grin, we set our sights on a daring new adventure—one that would see us delving into the murky depths of Arlington's lakes in search of lost treasures and a chance at golf ball salvation.

Keith Cox—what a character he was. We met as mere lads, thrown together by fate and the serendipity of schoolyard seating arrangements. I can still recall the day we first crossed paths at Clark Moore Middle School in '76, two misfits united by a shared love of mischief and a penchant for laughter.

It was Keith who first discovered my affinity for the game of golf—a discovery that would forever alter the course of our friendship. Eager to learn the ins and outs of the game, he approached me with a gleam in his eye and a determination that belied his tender years. And so, in the summer of '77, we found ourselves on the hallowed grounds of Arlington Country Club, where I assumed the role of mentor and Keith, with his natural athleticism and boundless enthusiasm, quickly proved himself a worthy pupil.

With each swing of the club, Keith's love for the game grew stronger, his passion igniting a fire within him that burned brighter with each passing day. And oh, how we played—morning, noon, and night, from sunup to sundown, our laughter ringing out across the fairways like a chorus of jubilant songbirds.

But it wasn't just Keith's skill on the course that endeared him to me—it was his irrepressible spirit, his infectious sense of humor, and his unwavering loyalty as a friend. He was a force of nature, a whirlwind of energy and enthusiasm, and being in his presence was like basking in the warm glow of a summer sunset.

And yet, as the years passed and we ventured into adulthood, life had a way of throwing us curveballs that we never saw coming. In February of 2001, Keith's light was extinguished far too soon, taken from us by the cruel hand of leukemia. And though he may be gone, his memory lives on in the laughter we shared, the adventures we embarked upon, and the bonds of friendship that transcend time and space.

So, here's to you, Keith Cox—a friend, a confidant, and a kindred spirit. May your laughter echo through the halls of eternity, a testament to the joy you brought into the lives of all who knew you.

In the summer of '79, Keith embarked on a new adventure, armed with nothing but a scuba diving certification and an insatiable thirst for exploration. With a wetsuit clinging to his frame like a second skin and a formidable underwater flashlight at his disposal, he was ready to plunge into the depths in search of lost treasures.

And so it was that we hatched a plan—one that would see Keith delving into the murky depths of Arlington's lakes while I patrolled the shoreline, a vigilant sentinel in search of stray golf balls. It was a partnership forged in the fires of friendship, a symbiotic relationship that promised to yield bountiful rewards for both parties involved.

With Keith navigating the depths and I scouring the shallows, we set about our task with the determination of seasoned explorers. Together, we would unearth enough golf balls to last us a lifetime—or at least until retirement beckoned with its siren song of leisurely rounds and sun-drenched fairways.

Oh, how we relished the prospect of our newfound enterprise, our imaginations running wild with visions of untold riches and boundless success. With each stroke of luck and every ball reclaimed from the depths, our confidence grew stronger, our resolve unshakeable in the face of adversity.

Yes, dear reader, we were a force to be reckoned with—a dynamic duo poised to conquer the watery depths and emerge victorious, our bags bulging with the spoils of our underwater conquests. And as we set out on our grand adventure, I couldn't help but feel a surge of excitement coursing through my veins, knowing that together, Keith and I were destined for greatness.

As we sauntered back to the pro shop, the prospect of facing Big Ray loomed large in our minds. But for Keith, negotiating with the seasoned golf pro was a walk in the park—a testament to his silver tongue and unwavering charm.

With a twinkle in his eye and a winning smile, Keith laid out our proposition to Big Ray with all the confidence of a seasoned diplomat. And to our delight, the grizzled veteran of the fairways proved more than amenable to our proposal, agreeing to a 50-50 split of the spoils without so much as a second thought.

Oh, how we celebrated our triumph, our hearts soaring with the thrill of victory as we envisioned the riches that awaited us. And as Big Ray issued his parting words of caution, warning us to finish our task before the morning golfers arrived, we nodded in solemn agreement, eager to prove ourselves equal to the challenge.

The anticipation of our upcoming adventure left us restless, our minds abuzz with excitement as we tossed and turned through the night. With Hefty Bags at the ready and Keith's scuba gear standing sentinel in the corner, we awaited the dawn with bated breath, eager to plunge headlong into the unknown depths of Arlington's lakes.

And so it was that we found ourselves back at Arlington in the wee hours of the morning, our spirits buoyed by the promise of adventure and the allure of hidden treasures waiting to be discovered. With the first light of dawn illuminating the horizon, we set to work with a fervor unmatched, our determination driving us forward as we raced against the clock to complete our mission.

Ah, Keith—there he stood, a picture of unbridled enthusiasm, his smile a beacon of hope in the darkness of the early morning hours. With his trusty flashlight in hand and his scuba fins at the ready, he was a vision of determination, his spirit undaunted by the challenges that lay ahead.

And oh, the audacity of it all! To think that we, mere mortals, would dare to tread where no man had tread before, defying the odds and challenging the status quo with every stroke of our paddles. Even Big Ray, with his gruff exterior and seasoned demeanor, couldn't help but be amused by our audaciousness, grudgingly conceding to leave a golf cart at our disposal as we set out on our grand expedition.

But little did he know that beneath our youthful bravado lay a steely resolve and a determination to succeed at any cost. For we were not just two punks out for a lark—we were pioneers, adventurers, intrepid explorers in search of lost treasures and hidden truths waiting to be unearthed.

And so, with the first light of dawn casting its golden glow upon the landscape, we set forth into the great unknown, our hearts brimming with hope and our spirits soaring with the promise of discovery. For in that moment, dear reader, we were more than just two boys on a mission—we were legends in the making, destined to leave our mark on the annals of Arlington Country Club and beyond.

As the first light of dawn cast its soft glow upon Arlington Country Club, we arrived with a sense of purpose that bordered on obsession. With the clock striking 4:00 AM, we wasted no time in setting our plan into motion, piling into the awaiting golf cart and making our way to the shores of the infamous fourth hole.

Dynamic Diving Duo: Donn and Keith 1979

With Keith donning his scuba gear and plunging into the murky depths below, I took to the shoreline with a sense of determination that bordered on desperation. Armed with nothing but a keen eye and a pair of steady hands, I scoured the shallows for any sign of our elusive quarry, my heart pounding with each discovery.

And oh, what a sight it was to behold! With each dive and each sweep of the shoreline, we unearthed a veritable treasure trove of lost golf balls—850 in all, to be precise—in the span of just three and a half hours. It was a feat of unparalleled daring, a testament to the power of friendship and the indomitable spirit of two boys on a mission.

The Stash

I can still recall the thrill of the hunt, the rush of adrenaline coursing through my veins as I reached down to pluck not one, not two, but three or four golf balls from the depths below. Meanwhile, Keith, with his scuba fins propelling him through the water like a sleek aquatic predator, surfaced time and time again, his arms laden with spoils as he tossed them onto the shore with reckless abandon.

And as we stood there, surrounded by a mountain of reclaimed golf balls, a sense of satisfaction washed over us—a feeling of redemption that transcended the mere act of collecting lost treasures. For in that moment, dear reader, we had achieved something far greater than we had ever imagined—a victory against the odds, a triumph of the human spirit, and a bond between friends that would endure for a lifetime.

As we stood there, the weight of our conquests straining against the seams of the Hefty Bags, a sense of unease began to creep into our minds. For in that moment, as I moved to load our spoils onto the waiting golf cart, Keith uttered words that would change everything.

"What are you doing?" he asked, his voice filled with a sense of urgency that caught me off guard. Confused, I explained that I was preparing to transport the golf balls to the pro shop, eager to divvy up our bounty with Big Ray as agreed.

But Keith had other ideas—ideas born from a sense of defiance and a determination to see our mission through to the end. With a steely glint in his eye, he proposed a daring plan: to stash the Hefty Bags beneath the fence that lined the perimeter of the course, ensuring our hard-won treasures remained hidden from prying eyes until the time was right.

And so it was that we found ourselves on the brink of deception, our hearts racing with the thrill of the forbidden and the fear of discovery. As Keith ventured forth to face Big Ray and negotiate our share of the spoils, I could do nothing but watch from afar, my nerves frayed and my conscience weighing heavy upon me.

But oh, the sweet taste of victory when Keith returned triumphant, his pockets bulging with a portion of our ill-gotten gains. For in that moment, dear reader, we had outwitted the odds and emerged victorious against all odds—a testament to the power of friendship, the allure of adventure, and the sheer audacity of two boys with a dream.

Big Ray may have felt a twinge of disappointment at his share of the spoils, but time has a way of softening even the keenest of disappointments. As for Keith and me, our deal may not have led to the grand redemption we had envisioned, but it certainly made a dent in our ever-dwindling supply of golf balls.

Divvying up those 750 golf balls was a task filled with laughter and camaraderie, a reminder of the countless hours we had spent together on the links, chasing after dreams that seemed just out of reach. Yet, as life inevitably pulled us in different directions, our opportunities to play together grew fewer and farther between until they were but fleeting moments in the tapestry of our lives.

Yes, dear reader, it was a moment of triumph—a victory won through cunning negotiation and unwavering resolve. And as we made our triumphant return to the clubhouse, our bags brimming with reclaimed golf balls, I couldn't help but marvel at the sheer audacity of it all. Truly, there are few things in life more satisfying than outsmarting Big Ray at his own game.

I'll never forget our last round together in Omaha, the sun setting on a day filled with memories both cherished and bittersweet. And though Keith may no longer walk this earth beside me, his spirit lives on in the echoes of our laughter and the bond of friendship that transcends the boundaries of time and space.

In his memory, I've pledged to share our story with the world, to honor the legacy of a dear friend and a life lived with passion and purpose. And so, I offer these words to you, dear reader, in the hope that they may serve as a testament to the enduring power of friendship, the joy of adventure, and the timeless allure of the game of golf.

For Keith, for Big Ray, for Arlington Country Club, and for the game itself—I raise my club in salute, knowing that their spirits will forever dwell in the hallowed halls of memory, where legends are born, and dreams take flight.

In loving memory of Keith Cox.

www.ingramcontent.com/pod-product-compliance
Lightning Source LLC
Chambersburg PA
CBHW041145110526
44590CB00027B/4125